THE LIFE OF THE SPIRIT AND THE LIFE OF TO-DAY

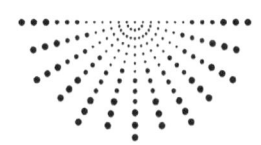

EVELYN UNDERHILL

ALICIA EDITIONS

CONTENTS

PREFACE 7
CHAPTER I 10
THE CHARACTERS OF SPIRITUAL LIFE
CHAPTER II 31
HISTORY AND THE LIFE OF THE SPIRIT
CHAPTER III 51
PSYCHOLOGY AND THE LIFE OF THE SPIRIT (I) THE ANALYSIS OF MIND
CHAPTER IV 72
PSYCHOLOGY AND THE LIFE OF THE SPIRIT (II) CONTEMPLATION AND SUGGESTION
CHAPTER V 95
INSTITUTIONAL RELIGION AND THE LIFE OF THE SPIRIT
CHAPTER VI 116
THE LIFE OF THE SPIRIT IN THE INDIVIDUAL
CHAPTER VII 137
THE LIFE OF THE SPIRIT AND EDUCATION
CHAPTER VIII 158
THE LIFE OF THE SPIRIT AND THE SOCIAL ORDER
PRINCIPAL WORKS USED OR CITED 177

Also by Evelyn Underhill 183

*Initio tu, Domine, terram fundasti; et opera manuum
   tuarum sunt caeli.
Ipsi peribunt, tu autem permanes; et omnes sicut
   vestimentum veterascent.
Et sicut opertorium mutabis eos, et mutabuntur;
Tu autem idem ipse es, et anni tui non deficient.
Filii servorum tuorum habitabunt; et semen eorum in
   seculum dirigetur.*

— PSALM CII: 25-28

PREFACE

This book owes its origin to the fact that in the autumn of 1921 the authorities of Manchester College, Oxford invited me to deliver the inaugural course of a lectureship in religion newly established under the will of the late Professor Upton. No conditions being attached to this appointment, it seemed a suitable opportunity to discuss, so far as possible in the language of the moment, some of the implicits which I believe to underlie human effort and achievement in the domain of the spiritual life. The material gathered for this purpose has now been added to, revised, and to some extent re-written, in order to make it appropriate to the purposes of the reader rather than the hearer. As the object of the book is strictly practical, a special attempt has been made to bring the classic experiences of the spiritual life into line with the conclusions of modern psychology, and in particular, to suggest some of the directions in which recent psychological research may cast light on the standard problems of the religious consciousness. This subject is still in its infancy; but it is destined, I am sure, in the near future to exercise a transforming influence on the study of spiritual experience, and may even prove to be the starting point of a new apologetic. Those who are inclined either to fear or to resent the application to this experience of those laws which—as we are now gradually discovering—govern the rest of our psychic life, or who are offended by the resulting demonstrations of continuity between our most homely and most lofty reactions to the universe, might take to themselves the plain words of Thomas à Kempis: "Thou art a man and not God, thou art flesh and no angel."

Since my subject is not the splendor of historic sanctity but the normal life of the Spirit, as it may be and is lived in the here-and-now, I have done my best to describe the character and meaning of this life in the ordinary terms of present day thought, and with little or no use of the technical language of mysticism. For the same reason, no attention has been given to those abnormal experiences and states of consciousness, which, too often regarded as specially "mystical," are now recognized by all competent students as representing the unfortunate accidents rather than the abiding substance of spirituality. Readers of these pages will find nothing about trances, Ecstasies and other rare psychic phenomena; which sometimes indicate holiness, and sometimes only disease. For information on these matters they must go to larger and more technical works. My aim here is the more general one, of indicating first the characteristic experiences—discoverable within all great religions—which justify or are fundamental to the spiritual life, and the way in which these experiences may be accommodated to the world-view of the modern man: and next, the nature of that spiritual life as it appears in human history. The succeeding sections of the book treat in some detail the light cast on spiritual problems by mental analysis—a process which need not necessarily be conducted from the standpoint of a degraded materialism—and by recent work on the psychology of autistic thought and of suggestion. These investigations have a practical interest for every man who desires to be the "captain of his soul." The relation in which institutional religion does or should stand to the spiritual life is also in part a matter for psychology; which is here called upon to deal with the religious aspect of the social instincts, and the problems surrounding symbols and cults. These chapters lead up to a discussion of the personal aspect of the spiritual life, its curve of growth, characters and activities; and a further section suggests some ways in which educationists might promote the up springing of this life in the young. Finally, the last chapter attempts to place the fact of the life of the Spirit in its relation to the social order, and to indicate some of the results which might follow upon its healthy corporate development. It is superfluous to point out that each of these subjects needs, at least, a volume to itself: and to some of them I shall hope to return in the future. Their treatment in the present work is necessarily fragmentary and suggestive; and is intended rather to stimulate thought, than to offer solutions.

Part of Chapter IV has already appeared in "The Fortnightly Review" under the title "Suggestion and Religious Experience." Chapter VIII incorporates several passages from an article on "Sources of Power in Human Life" originally contributed to the "Hubert Journal." These are reprinted by kind permission of the editors concerned. My numerous debts to previous writers are obvious, and for the most part are acknowledged in the footnotes; the greatest, to the works of Baron Von Hugely, will be clear to all students of his writings. Thanks are also due to my old friend William Scott Palmer, who read part of the manuscript and gave me much generous and valuable advice. It is a pleasure to express in this place my warm gratitude first to the Principal and authorities of Manchester College, who gave me the opportunity of delivering these chapters in their original form, and whose unfailing sympathy and kindness so greatly helped me: and secondly, to the members of the Oxford Faculty of Theology, to whom I owe the great Honor of being the first woman lecturer in religion to appear in the University list.

E.U.
Epiphany, 1922.

CHAPTER I

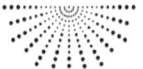

THE CHARACTERS OF SPIRITUAL LIFE

This book has been called "The Life of the Spirit and the Life of To-day" in order to emphasize as much as possible the practical, here-and-now nature of its subject; and specially to combat the idea that the spiritual life—or the mystic life, as its more intense manifestations are sometimes called—is to be regarded as primarily a matter of history. It is not. It is a matter of biology. Though we cannot disregard history in our study of it, that history will only be valuable to us in so far as we keep tight hold on its direct connection with the present, its immediate bearing on our own lives: and this we shall do only in so far as we realize the unity of all the higher experiences of the race. In fact, were I called upon to choose a motto which should express the central notion of these chapters, that motto would be—"There are diversities of gifts, but the same Spirit." This declaration I would interpret in the widest possible sense; as suggesting the underlying harmony and single inspiration of all man's various and apparently conflicting expressions of his instinct for fullness of life. For we shall not be able to make order, in any hopeful sense, of the tangle of material which is before us, until we have subdued it to this ruling thought: seen one transcendent Object towards which all our twisting pathways run, and one impulsion pressing us towards it.

As psychology is now teaching us to find, at all levels of our craving, dreaming, or thinking, the diverse expressions of one psychic energy; so that type of philosophy which comes nearest to the religion of the Spirit,

THE LIFE OF THE SPIRIT AND THE LIFE OF TO-DAY

invites us to find at all levels of life the workings and strivings of one Power: "a Reality which both underlies and crowns all our other, lesser strivings."[1] Variously manifested in partial achievements of order and goodness, in diversities of beauty, and in our graded apprehensions of truth, this Spirit is yet most fully known to us in the transcendent values of holiness and love. The more deeply it is loved by man, the nearer he draws to its heart: and the greater his love, the more fully does he experience its transforming and energizing power. The words of Plotinus are still true for every one of us, and are unaffected by the presence or absence of creed:

"Yonder is the true object of our love, which it is possible to grasp and to live with and truly to possess, since no envelope of flesh separates us from it. He who has seen it knows what I say, that the soul then has another life, when it comes to God, and having come possesses Him, and knows when in that state that it is in the presence of the dispenser of true life and that it needs nothing further."[2]

So, if we would achieve anything like a real integration of life—and until we have done so, we are bound to be restless and uncertain in our touch upon experience—we are compelled to press back towards contact with this living Reality, however conceived by us. And this not by way of a retreat from our actual physical and mental life, but by way of a fulfilment of it.

More perhaps than ever before, men are now driven to ask themselves the searching question of the disciple in Boehme's Dialogue on the Supersensual Life: "Seeing I am in nature, how may I come through nature into the supersensual ground, without destroying nature?"[3] And such a coming through into the ground, such a finding and feeling of Eternal Life, is I take it the central business of religion. For religion is committed to achieving a synthesis of the eternal and the ever-fleeting, of nature and of spirit; lifting up the whole of life to a greater reality, because a greater participation in eternity. Such a participation in eternity, manifested in the time-world, is the very essence of the spiritual life: but, set as we are in mutability, our apprehensions of it can only be partial and relative. Absolutes are known only to absolute mind; our measurements, however careful and intricate, can never tally with the measurements of God. As Einstein conceives of space curved round the sun we, borrowing his symbolism for a moment, may perhaps think of the world of Spirit as curved round the human soul; shaped to our finite understanding, and therefore presenting to us innumerable angles of approach. This means that God can and must be sought only within and through our human experience. "Where," says Jacob Boehme, "will you seek for God? Seek Him in your soul, which has proceeded out of the Eternal Nature, the living fountain of forces wherein the Divine working stands."[4]

But, on the other hand, such limitation as this is no argument for agnosticism. For this our human experience in its humbling imperfection, however we interpret it, is as real within its own system of reference as anything else. It is our inevitably limited way of laying hold on the stuff of existence: and not less real for that than the monkeys' way on one hand, or the angels' way on the other. Only we must be sure that we do it as thoroughly and completely as we can; disdaining the indolence which so easily relapses to the lower level and the smaller world.

And the first point I wish to make is, that the experience which we call the life of the Spirit is such a genuine fact; which meets us at all times and places, and at all levels of life. It is an experience which is independent of, and often precedes, any explanation or rationalization we may choose to make of it: and no one, as a matter of fact, takes any real interest in the explanation, unless he has had some form of the experience. We notice, too, that it is most ordinarily and also most impressively given to us as such an objective experience, whole and unanalyzed; and that when it is thus given, and perceived as effecting a transfiguration of human character, we on our part most readily understand and respond to it.

Thus Plotinus, than whom few persons have lived more capable of analysis, can only say: "The soul knows when in that state that it is in the presence of the dispenser of true life." Yet in saying this, does he not tell us far more, and rouse in us a greater and more fruitful longing, than in all his disquisitions about the worlds of Spirit and of Soul? And Kabir, from another continent and time, saying "More than all else do I cherish at heart the love which makes me to live a limitless life in this world,"[5] assures us in these words that he too has known that more abundant life. These are the statements of the pure religious experience, in so far as "pure" experience is possible to us; which is only of course in a limited and relative sense. The subjective element, all that the psychologist means by apperception, must enter in, and control it. Nevertheless, they refer to man's communion with an independent objective Reality. This experience is more real and concrete, therefore more important, than any of the systems by which theology seeks to explain it. We may then take it, without prejudice to any special belief, that the spiritual life we wish to study is *one life*; based on experience of one Reality, and manifested in the diversity of gifts and graces which men have been willing to call true, holy, beautiful and good. For the moment at least we may accept the definition of it given by Dr. Bosanquet, as "oneness with the Supreme Good in every facet of the heart and will."[6] And since without derogation of its transcendent character, its vigour, wonder and worth, it is in human experience rather than in speculation that we are bound to seek it, we shall look first at the forms taken by man's intuition of Eternity, the life to which it seems to call him; and next at the actual appearance of this life in history. Then at the psychological machinery by which we may lay hold of it, the contributions which religious institutions make to its realization; and last, turning our backs on these partial explorations of the living Whole, seek if we can to seize something of its inwardness as it appears to the individual, the way in which education may best prepare its fulfilment, and the part it must play in the social group.

We begin therefore at the starting point of this life of Spirit: in man's vague, fluctuating, yet persistent apprehension of an enduring and transcendent reality—his instinct for God. The characteristic forms taken by this instinct are simple and fairly well known. Complication only comes in with the interpretation we put on them.

By three main ways we tend to realize our limited personal relations with that transcendent Other which we call divine, eternal or real; and these, appearing perpetually in the vast literature of religion, might be illustrated from all places and all times.

First, there is the profound sense of security: of being safely held in a cosmos of which, despite all contrary appearance, peace is the very heart, and which is not inimical to our true interests. For those whose religious experience takes this form, God is the Ground of the soul, the Unmoved, our Very Rest; statements which meet us again and again in spiritual literature. This certitude of a principle of permanence within and beyond our world of change—the sense of Eternal Life—lies at the very centre of the religious consciousness; which will never on this point capitulate to the attacks of philosophy on the one hand (such as those of the New Realists) or of psychology on the other hand, assuring him that what he mistakes for the Eternal World is really his own unconscious mind. Here man, at least in his great representatives—the persons of transcendent religious genius—seems to get beyond all labels. He finds and feels a truth that cannot fail him, and that satisfies both his heart and mind; a justification of that transcendental feeling which is the soul alike of philosophy and of art. If his life has its roots here, it will be a fruitful tree; and whatever its outward activities, it will be a spiritual life, since it is lived, as George Fox was so fond of saying, in the Universal Spirit. All know the great passage In St. Augustine's Confessions in which he describes how "the mysterious eye of his soul gazed on the Light that never changes; above the eye of the soul, and above intelligence."[7] There is nothing archaic in such an experience. Though its description may depend on the language of Neoplatonism, it is in its essence as possible and as fruitful for us to-day as it was in the fourth century, and the doctrine and discipline of Christian prayer have always admitted its validity.

Here and in many other examples which might be quoted, the spiritual fact is interpreted in a non-personal and cosmic way; and we must remember that what is described to us is always, inevitably, the more or less emotional interpretation, never the pure immediacy of experience. This interpretation frequently makes use of the symbolisms of space, stillness, and light: the contemplative soul is "lost in the ocean of the Godhead," "enters His silence" or exclaims with Dante:

> *"la mia vista, venendo sincera,*
> *e più e più entrava per lo raggio*
> *dell' alta luce, che da sè è vera."*[8]

But in the second characteristic form of the religious experience, the relationship is felt rather as the intimate and reciprocal communion of a person with a Person; a form of apprehension which is common to the great majority of devout natures. It is true that Divine Reality, while doubtless including in its span all the values we associate with personality, must far overpass it: and this conclusion has been reached again and again by profoundly religious minds, of whom among Christians we need only mention Dionysius the Areopagite, Eckhart, and Ruysbroeck. Yet these very minds have always in the end discovered the necessity of finding place for the overwhelming certitude of a personal contact, a prevenient and an answering love. For it is always in a personal and emotional relationship that man finds himself impelled to surrender to God; and this surrender is felt by him to evoke a response. It is significant that even modern liberalism is forced, in the teeth of rationality, to acknowledge this fact of the religious experience. Thus we have on the one hand the Catholic-minded but certainly unorthodox Spanish thinker, Miguel de Unamuno, confessing—

"I believe in God as I believe in my friends, because I feel the breath of His affection, feel His invisible and intangible hand, drawing me, leading me, grasping me.... Once and again in my life I have seen myself suspended in a trance over the abyss; once and again I have found myself at the cross-roads, confronted by a choice of ways and aware that in choosing one I should be renouncing all the others—for there is no turning back upon these roads of life; and once and again in such unique moments as these I have felt the impulse of a mighty power, conscious, sovereign and loving. And then, before the feet of the wayfarer, opens out the way of the Lord."[9]

Compare with this Upton the Unitarian: "If," he says, "this Absolute Presence, which meets us face to face in the most momentous of our life's experiences, which pours into our fainting the elixir of new life-mud strength, and into our wounded hearts the balm of a quite infinite sympathy, cannot fitly be called a personal presence, it is only because this word personal is too poor and carries with it associations too human and too limited adequately to express this profound God-consciousness."[10]

Such a personal God-consciousness is the one impelling cause of those moral struggles, sacrifices and purifications, those costing and heroic activities, to which all greatly spiritual souls find themselves drawn. We note that these souls experience it even when it conflicts with their philosophy: for a real religious intuition is always accepted by the self that has it as taking priority of thought, and carrying with it so to speak its own guarantees. Thus Blake, for whom the Holy Ghost was an "intellectual fountain," hears the Divine Voice crying:

> *"I am not a God afar off, I am a brother and friend;*
> *Within your bosoms I reside, and you reside in me."*[11]

Thus in the last resort the Sufi poet can only say:

> *"O soul, seek the Beloved; O friend, seek the Friend!"*[12]

Thus even Plotinus is driven to speak of his Divine Wisdom as the Father and ever-present Companion of the soul,[13] and Kabir, for whom God is the Unconditioned and the Formless, can yet exclaim:

"From the beginning until the end of time there is love between me and thee: and how shall such love be extinguished?"[14]

Christianity, through its concepts of the Divine Fatherhood and of the Eternal Christ, has given to this sense of personal communion its fullest and most beautiful expression:

> *"Amore, chi t'ama non sta ozioso,*
> *tanto li par dolce de te gustare,*
> *ma tutta ora vive desideroso*
> *como te possa stretto piú amare;*
> *ché tanto sta per te lo cor gioioso,*
> *chi nol sentisse, nol porría parlare*
> *quanto é dolce a gustare lo tuo sapore."[15]*

On the immense question of *what* it is that lies behind this sense of direct intercourse, this passionate friendship with the Invisible, I cannot enter. But it has been one of the strongest and most fruitful influences in religious history, and gives in particular its special colour to the most perfect developments of Christian mysticism.

Last—and here is the aspect of religious experience which is specially to concern us—Spirit is felt as an inflowing power, a veritable accession of vitality; energizing the self, or the religious group, impelling it to the fullest and most zealous living-out of its existence, giving it fresh joy and vigour, and lifting it to fresh levels of life. This sense of enhanced life is a mark of all religions of the Spirit. "He giveth power to the faint," says the Second Isaiah, "and to them that hath no might he increaseth strength ... they that wait upon the Lord shall renew their strength; they shall mount up with wings as eagles; they shall run and not be weary; and they shall walk, and not faint."[16] "I live—yet not I," "I can do all things," says St. Paul, seeking to express his dependence on this Divine strength invading and controlling him: and assures his neophytes that they too have received "the Spirit of power." "My life," says St. Augustine, "shall be a real life, being wholly full of Thee."[17] "Having found God," says a modern Indian saint, "the current of my life flowed on swiftly, I gained fresh strength."[18] All other men and women of the Spirit speak in the same sense, when they try to describe the source of their activity and endurance.

So, the rich experiences of the religious consciousness seem to be resumed in these three outstanding types of spiritual awareness. The cosmic, ontological, or transcendent; finding God as the infinite Reality outside and beyond us. The personal, finding Him as the living and responsive object of our love, in immediate touch with us. The dynamic, finding Him as the power that dwells within or energizes us. These are not exclusive but complementary apprehensions, giving objectives to intellect feeling and will. They must all be taken into account in any attempt to estimate the full character of the spiritual life, and this life can hardly achieve perfection unless all three be present in some measure. Thus the French contemplative Lucie-Christine says, that when the voice of God called her it was at one and the same time a Light, a Drawing, and a Power,[19] and her Indian contemporary the Maharishi Devendranath Tagore, that "Seekers after God must realize Brahma in these three places. They must see Him within, see Him without, and see Him in that abode of Brahma where He exists in Himself."[20] And it seems to me, that what we have in the Christian doctrine of the Trinity, is above all the crystallization and mind's interpretation of these three ways in which our simple contact with God is actualized by us. It is, like so many other dogmas when we get to the bottom of them, an attempt to describe experience. What is that supernal symphony of which this elusive music, with its three complementary strains, forms part? We cannot know this, since we are debarred by our situation from knowledge of wholes. But even those strains which we do hear, assure us how far we are yet from conceiving the possibilities of life, of power, of beauty which are contained in them.

And if the first type of experience, with the immense feeling of assurance, of peace, and of quietude which comes from our intuitive contact with that world which Ruysbroeck called the "world that is unwalled,"[21] and from the mind's utter surrender and abolition of resistances—if all this seems to lead to a merely static or contemplative conception of the spiritual life; the third type of experience, with its impulse towards action, its often strongly felt accession of vitality and power, leads inevitably to a complementary and dynamic interpretation of that life. Indeed, if the first moment in the life of the Spirit be man's apprehension of Eternal Life, the second moment—without which the first has little worth for him—consists of his response to that transcendent Reality. Perception of it lays on him the obligation of living in its atmosphere, fulfilling its meaning, if he can: and this will involve for him a measure of inward transformation, a difficult growth and change. Thus the ideas of new birth and regeneration have always been, and I think must ever be, closely associated with man's discovery of God: and the soul's true path seems to be from intuition, through adoration, to moral effort, and thence to charity.

Even so did the Oxford Methodists, who began by trying only to worship God and *be* good by adhering to a strict devotional rule, soon find themselves impelled to try to *do* good by active social work.[22] And at his highest development, and in so far as he has appropriated the full richness of experience which is offered to him, man will and should find himself, as it were, flung to and fro between action and contemplation. Between the call to transcendence, to a simple self-loss in the unfathomable and adorable life of God, and the call to a full, rich and various actualization of personal life, in the energetic strivings of a fellow worker with Him: between the soul's profound sense of transcendent love, and its felt possession of and duty towards immanent love—a paradox which only some form of incarnational philosophy can solve. It is said of Abu Said, the great Sūfi, at the full term of his development, that he "did all normal things while ever thinking of God."[23] Here, I believe, we find the norm of the spiritual life, in such a complete response both to the temporal and to the eternal revelations and demands of the Divine nature: on the one hand, the highest and most costing calls made on us by that world of succession in which we find ourselves; on the other, an unmoved abiding in the bosom of eternity, "where was never heard quarter-clock to strike, never seen minute glasse to turne."[24]

There have been many schools and periods in which one half of this dual life of man has been unduly emphasized to the detriment of the other. Often in the East—and often too in the first, pre-Benedictine phase of Christian monasticism—there has been an unbalanced cultivation of the contemplative life, resulting in a narrow, abnormal, imperfectly vitalized a-social type of spirituality. On the other hand, in our own day the tendency to action usually obliterates the contemplative side of experience altogether: and the result is the feverishness, exhaustion and uncertainty of aim characteristic of the over-driven and the underfed. But no one can be said to live in its fulness the life of the Spirit who does not observe a due balance between the two: both receiving and giving, both apprehending and expressing, and thus achieving that state of which Ruysbroeck said "Then only is our life a whole, when work and contemplation dwell in us side by side, and we are perfectly in both of them at once."[25] All Christian writers on the life of the Spirit point to the perfect achievement of this two-fold ideal in Christ; the pattern of that completed humanity towards which the indwelling Spirit is pressing the race. His deeds of power and mercy, His richly various responses to every level of human existence, His gift to others of new faith and life, were directly dependent on the nights spent on the mountain in prayer. When St. Paul entreats us to grow up into the fulness of His stature, this is the ideal that is implied.

In the intermediate term of the religious experience, that felt communion with a Person which is the *clou* of the devotional life, we get as it were the link between the extreme apprehensions of transcendence and of immanence, and their expression in the lives of contemplation and of action; and also a focus for that religious-emotion which is the most powerful stimulus to spiritual growth. It is needless to emphasize the splendid use which Christianity has made of this type of experience; nor unfortunately, the exaggerations to which it has led. Both extremes are richly represented in the literature of mysticism. But we should remember that Christianity is not alone in thus requiring place to be made for such a conception of God as shall give body to all the most precious and fruitful experiences of the heart, providing simple human sense and human feeling with something on which to lay hold. In India, there is the existence, within and alongside the austere worship of the unconditioned Brahma, of the ardent personal Vaishnavite devotion to the heart's Lord, known as Bhakti Marga. In Islam, there is the impassioned longing of the Sūfis for the Beloved, who is "the Rose of all Reason and all Truth."

> *"Without Thee, O Beloved, I cannot rest;*
> *Thy goodness towards me I cannot reckon.*
> *Tho' every hair on my body becomes a tongue*
> *A thousandth part of the thanks due to Thee I cannot tell."*[26]

There is the sudden note of rapture which startles us in the Neoplatonists, as when Plotinus speaks of "the name of love for what is there to know—the passion of the lover testing on the 'bosom of his love.'"[27] Surely we may accept all these, as the instinctive responses of a diversity of spirits to the one eternal Spirit of life and love: and recognize that without such personal response, such a discovery of imperishable love, a fully lived spiritual life is no more possible than is a fully lived physical life from which love has been left out.

When we descend from experience to interpretation, the paradoxical character of such a personal sense of intimacy is eased for us, if we remember that the religious man's awareness of the indwelling Spirit, or of a Divine companionship—whatever name he gives it—is just his limited realization, achieved by means of his own mental machinery, of a universal and not a particular truth. To this realization he brings all his human—more, his sub-human—feelings and experiences: not only those which are vaguely called his spiritual intuitions, but the full weight of his impulsive and emotional life. His experience and its interpretation are, then, inevitably conditioned by this apperceiving mass. And here I think the intellect should show mercy, and not probe without remorse into those tender places where the heart and the spirit are at one. Let us then be content to note, that when we consult the works of those who have best and most fully interpreted their religion in a universal sense, we find how careful they are to provide a category for this experience of a personally known and loved indwelling Divinity—man's Father, Lover, Saviour, ever-present Companion—which shall avoid its identification with the mere spirit of Nature, whilst safeguarding its immanence no less than its transcendent quality. Thus, Julian of Norwich heard in her meditations the voice of God saying to her, "See! I am in all things! See! I lift never mine hand from off my works, nor ever shall!"[28] Is it possible to state more plainly the indivisible identity of the Spirit of Life? "See! I am in *all* things!" In the terrific energies of the stellar universe, and the smallest song of the birds. In the seething struggle of modern industrialism, as much a part of nature, of those works on which His hands are laid, as the more easily comprehended economy of the ant-heap and the hive. This sense of the personal presence of an abiding Reality, fulfilling and transcending all our highest values, here in our space-time world of effort, may well be regarded as the differential mark of real spiritual experience, wherever found. It chimes well with the definition of Professor Pratt, who observes that the truly spiritual man, though he may not be any better morally than his non-religious neighbour, "has a confidence in the universe and an inner joy which the other does not know—is more at-home in the universe as a whole, than other men."[29]

If, in their attempt to describe their experience of this companioning Reality, spiritual men of all types have exhausted all the resources and symbols of poetry, even earthly lovers are obliged to do that, in order to suggest a fraction of the values contained in earthly love. Such a divine presence is dramatized for Christianity in the historic incarnation, though not limited by it: and it is continued into history by the beautiful Christian conception of the eternal indwelling Christ. The distinction made by the Bhakti form of Hinduism between the Manifest and the Unmanifest God seeks to express this same truth; and shows that this idea, in one form or another, is a necessity for religious thought.

Further and detailed illustration of spiritual experience in itself, as a genuine and abiding human fact—a form of life—independent of the dogmatic interpretations put on it, will come up as we proceed. I now wish to go on to a second point: this—that it follows that any complete description of human life as we know it, must find room for the spiritual factor, and for that religious life and temper in which it finds expression. This place must be found, not merely in the phenomenal series, as we might find room for any special human activity or aberration, from the medicine-man to the Jumping Perfectionists; but deep-set in the enduring stuff of man's true life. We must believe that the union of this life with supporting Spirit cannot *in fact* be broken, any more than the organic unity of the earth with the universe as a whole. But the extent in which we find and feel it is the measure of the fullness of spiritual life that we enjoy. Organic union must be lifted to conscious realization: and this to do, is the business of religion. In this act of realization each aspect of the psychic life—thought, will and feeling—must have its part, and from each must be evoked a response. Only in so far as such all-round realization and response are achieved by us do we live the spiritual life. We do it perhaps in some degree, every time that we surrender to pure beauty or unselfish devotion; for then all but the most insensitive must be conscious of an unearthly touch, and hear the cadence of a heavenly melody. In these partial experiences something, as it were, of the richness of Reality overflows and is experienced by us. But it is in the wholeness of response characteristic of religion—that uncalculated response to stimulus which is the mark of the instinctive life—that this Realty of love and power is most truly found and felt by us. In this generous and heart-searching surrender of religion, rightly made, the self achieves inner harmony, and finds a satisfying objective for all its cravings and energies. It then finds its life, and the possibilities before it, to be far greater than it knew.

We need not claim that those men and women who have most fully realized, and so at first hand have described to us, this life of the Spirit, have neither discerned or communicated the ultimate truth of things; nor need we claim that the symbols they use have intrinsic value, beyond the poetic power of suggesting to us the quality and wonder of their transfigured lives. Still less must we claim this discovery as the monopoly of any one system of religion. But we can and ought to claim, that no system shall be held satisfactory which does not find a place for it: and that only in so far as we at least apprehend and respond to the world's spiritual aspect, do we approach the full stature of humanity. Psychologists at present are much concerned to entreat us to "face reality," discarding idealism along with the other phantasies that haunt the race. Yet this facing of reality can hardly be complete if we do not face the facts of the spiritual life. Certainly we shall find it most difficult to interpret these facts; they are confused, and more than one reading of them is possible. But still we cannot leave them out and claim to have "faced reality."

Höffding goes so far as to say that any real religion implies and must give us a world-view.[30] And I think it is true that any vividly lived spiritual life must, as soon as it passes beyond the level of mere feeling and involves reflection, involve too some more or less articulated conception of the spiritual universe, in harmony with which that life is to be lived. This may be given to us by authority, in the form of creed: but if we do not thus receive it, we are committed to the building of our own City of God. And to-day, that world-view, that spiritual landscape, must harmonize—if it is needed to help our living—with the outlook, the cosmic map, of the ordinary man. If it be adequate, it will inevitably transcend this; but must not be in hopeless conflict with it. The stretched-out, graded, striving world of biological evolution, the many-faced universe of the physical relativist, the space-time manifold of realist philosophy—these great constructions of human thought, so often ignored by the religious mind, must on the contrary be grasped, and accommodated to the world-view which centres on the God known in religious experience. They are true within their own systems of reference; and the soul demands a synthesis wide enough to contain them.

It is true that most religious systems, at least of the traditional type, do purport to give us a world-view, a universe, in which devotional experience is at home and finds an objective and an explanation. They give us a self-consistent symbolic world in which to live. But it is a world which is almost unrelated to the universe of modern physics, and emerges in a very dishevelled state from the explorations of history and of psychology. Even contrasted with our every-day unresting strenuous life, it is rather like a conservatory in a wilderness. Whilst we are inside everything seems all right.

Beauty and fragrance surround us. But emerging from its doors, we find ourselves meeting the cold glances of those who deal in other kinds of reality; and discover that such spiritual life as we possess has got to accommodate itself to the conditions in which they live. If the claim of religion be true at all, it is plain that the conservatory-type of spiritual world is inconsistent with it. Imperfect though any conception we frame of the universe must be—and here we may keep in mind Samuel Butler's warning that "there is no such source of error as the pursuit of absolute truth"—still, a view which is controlled by the religious factor ought to be, so to speak, a hill-top view. Lifting us up to higher levels, it ought to give us a larger synthesis. Hence, the wider the span of experience which we are able to bring within our system, the more valid its claim becomes: and the setting apart of spiritual experience in a special compartment, the keeping of it under glass, is daily becoming less possible. That experience is life in its fullness, or nothing at all. Therefore it must come out into the open, and must witness to its own most sacred conviction; that the universe as a whole is a religious fact, and man is not living completely until he is living in a world religiously conceived.

More and more, as it seems to me, philosophy moves toward this reading of existence. The revolt from the last century's materialism is almost complete. In religious language, abstract thought is again finding and feeling God within the world; and finding too in this discovery and realization the meaning, and perhaps—if we may dare to use such a word—the purpose of life. It suggests—and here, more and more, psychology supports it—that, real and alive as we are in relation to this system with which we find ourselves in correspondence, yet we are not so real, nor so alive, as it is possible to be. The characters of our psychic life point us on and up to other levels. Already we perceive that man's universe is no fixed order; and that the many ways in which he is able to apprehend it are earnests of a greater transfiguration, a more profound contact with reality yet possible to him. Higher forms of realization, a wider span of experience, a sharpening of our vague, uncertain consciousness of value—these may well be before us. We have to remember how dim, tentative, half-understood a great deal of our so-called "normal" experience is: how narrow the little field of consciousness, how small the number of impressions it picks up from the rich flux of existence, how subjective the picture it constructs from them. To take only one obvious example, artists and poets have given us plenty of hints that a real beauty and significance which we seldom notice lie at our very doors; and forbid us to contradict the statement of religion that God is standing there too.

That thought which inspires the last chapters of Professor 'Alexander's "Space, Time, and Deity," that the universe as a whole has a tendency towards deity, does at least seem true of the fully awakened human consciousness.[31] Though St. Thomas Aquinas may not have covered all the facts when he called man a contemplative animal,[32] he came nearer the mark than more modern anthropologists. Man has an ineradicable impulse to transcendence, though sometimes—as we may admit—it is expressed in strange ways: and no psychology which fails to take account of it can be accepted by us as complete. He has a craving which nothing in his material surroundings seems adequate either to awaken or to satisfy; a deep conviction that some larger synthesis of experience is possible to him. The sense that we are not yet full grown has always haunted the race. "I am the Food of the full-grown. *Grow,* and thou shalt feed on Me!"[33] said the voice of supreme Reality to St. Augustine. Here we seem to lay our finger on the distinguishing mark of humanity: that in man the titanic craving for a fuller life and love which is characteristic of all living things, has a teleological objective. He alone guesses that he may or should be something other; yet cannot guess what he may be. And from this vague sense of being *in via,* the restlessness and discord of his nature proceed. In him, the onward thrust of the world of becoming achieves self-consciousness.

The best individuals and communities of each age have felt this craving and conviction; and obeyed, in a greater or less degree, its persistent onward push. "The seed of the new birth," says William Law, "is not a notion, but a real strong essential hunger, an attracting, a magnetic desire."[34] Over and over again, rituals have dramatized this, desire and saints have surrendered to it. The history of religion and philosophy is really the history of the profound human belief that we have faculties capable of responding to orders of truth which, did we apprehend them, would change the whole character of our universe; showing us reality from another angle, lit by another light. And time after time too—as we shall see, when we come to consider the testimony of history—favourable variations have arisen within the race and proved in their own persons that this claim is true. Often at the cost of great pain, sacrifice, and inward conflict they have broken their attachments to the narrow world of the senses: and this act of detachment has been repaid by a new, more lucid vision, and a mighty inflow of power. The principle of degrees assures us that such changed levels of consciousness and angles of approach may well involve introduction into a universe of new relations, which we are not competent to criticize.[35] This is a truth which should make us humble in our efforts to understand the difficult and too often paradoxical utterances of religious genius. It suggests the puzzlings of philosophers and theologians—and, I may add, of psychologists too—over experiences which they have not shared, are not of great authority for those whose object is to find the secret of the Spirit, and make it useful for life. Here, the only witnesses we can receive are, on the one part, the first-hand witnesses of experience, and on the other part, our own profound instinct that these are telling us news of our native land.

Baron von Hügel has finely said, that the facts of this spiritual life are themselves the earnests of its objective. These facts cannot be explained merely as man's share in the cosmic movement towards a yet unrealized

THE LIFE OF THE SPIRIT AND THE LIFE OF TO-DAY

perfection; such as the unachieved and self-evolving Divinity of some realist philosophers. "For we have no other instance of an unrealized perfection producing such pain and joy, such volitions, such endlessly varied and real results; and all by means of just this vivid and persistent impression that this Becoming is an already realized Perfection."[36] Therefore though the irresistible urge and the effort forward, experienced on highest levels of love and service, are plainly one-half of the life of the Spirit—which can never be consistent with a pious indolence, an acceptance of things as they are, either in the social or the individual life—yet, the other half, and the very inspiration of that striving, is this certitude of an untarnishable Perfection, a great goal really there; a living God Who draws all spirits to Himself. "Our quest," said Plotinus, "is of an End, not of ends: for that only can be chosen by us which is ultimate and noblest, that which calls forth the tenderest longings of our soul."[37]

There is of course a sense in which such a life of the Spirit is the same yesterday, to-day and for ever. Even if we consider it in relation to historical time, the span within which it has appeared is so short, compared with the ages of human evolution, that we may as well regard it as still in the stage of undifferentiated infancy. Yet even babies change, and change quickly, in their relations with the external world. And though the universe with which man's childish spirit is in contact be a world of enduring values; yet, placed as we are in the stream of succession, part of the stuff of a changing world and linked at every point with it, our apprehensions of this life of spirit, the symbols we use to describe it—and we must use symbols—must inevitably change too. Therefore from time to time some restatement becomes imperative, if actuality is not to be lost. Whatever God meant man to do or to be, the whole universe assures us that He did not mean him to stand still. Such a restatement, then, may reasonably be called a truly religious work; and I believe that it is indeed one of the chief works to which religion must find itself committed in the near future. Hence my main object In this book is to recommend the consideration of this enduring fact of the life of the Spirit and what it can mean to us, from various points of view; thus helping to prepare the ground for that synthesis which we may not yet be able to achieve, but towards which we ought to look. It is from this stand-point, and with this object of examining what we have, of sorting out if we can the permanent from the transitory, of noticing lacks and bridging cleavages, that we shall consider in turn the testimony of history, the position in respect of psychology, and the institutional personal and social aspects of the spiritual life.

In such a restatement, such a reference back to actual man, here at the present day as we have him—such a demand for a spiritual interpretation of the universe, which will allow us to fit in all his many-levelled experiences—I believe we have the way of approach to which religion to-day must look as its best hope. Thus only can we conquer that museum-like atmosphere of much traditional piety which—agreeable as it may be to the historic or æsthetic sense—makes it so unreal to our workers, no less than to our students. Such a method, too, will mean the tightening of that alliance between philosophy and psychology which is already a marked character of contemporary thought.

And note that, working on this basis, we need not in order to find room for the facts commit ourselves to the harsh dualism, the opposition between nature and spirit, which is characteristic of some earlier forms of Christian thought. In this dualism, too, we find simply an effort to describe felt experience. It is an expression of the fact, so strongly and deeply felt by the richest natures, that there *is* an utter difference in kind between the natural life of use and wont, as most of us live it, and the life that is dominated by the spiritual consciousness. The change is indeed so great, the transfiguration so complete, that they seize on the strongest language in which to state it. And in the good old human way, referring their own feelings to the universe, they speak of the opposing and incompatible worlds of matter and of spirit, of nature and of grace. But those who have most deeply reflected, have perceived that the change effected is not a change of worlds. It is rather such a change of temper and attitude as will disclose within our one world, here and now, the one Spirit in the diversity of His gifts; the one Love, in homeliest incidents as well as noblest vision, laying its obligations on the soul; and so the true nature and full possibilities of this our present life.

Although it is true that we must register our profound sense of the transcendental character of this spirit-life, its otherness from mere nature, and the humility and penitence in which alone mere nature receive it; yet I think that our movement from one to the other is more naturally described by us in the language of growth than in the language of convulsion. The primal object of religion is to disclose to us this perdurable basis of life, and foster our growth into communion with it. And whatever its special, language and personal colour be—for all our news of God comes to us through the consciousness of individual men, and arrives tinctured by their feelings and beliefs—in the end it does this by disclosing us to ourselves as spirits growing up, though unevenly and hampered by our past, through the physical order into completeness of response to a universe that is itself a spiritual fact. "Heaven," said Jacob Boehme, "is nothing else but a manifestation of the Eternal One, wherein all worketh and willeth in quiet love."[38] Such a manifestation of Spirit must clearly be made through humanity, at least so far as our own order is concerned: by our redirection and full use of that spirit of life which energizes us, and which, emerging from the more primitive levels of organic creation, is ours to carry on and up—either to new self-satisfactions, or to new consecrations.

It is hardly worth while to insist that the need for such a redirection has never been more strongly felt than at the present day. There is indeed no period in which history exhibits mankind as at once more active, more feverishly self-conscious, and more distracted, than is our own bewildered generation; nor any which stood in greater need of Blake's exhortation: "Let every Christian as much as in him lies, engage himself openly and publicly before all the World in some Mental pursuit for the Building up of Jerusalem."[39]

How many people do each of us know who work and will in quiet love, and thus participate in eternal life?

Consider the weight of each of these words. The energy, the clear purpose, the deep calm, the warm charity they imply. Willed work; not grudging toil. Quiet love, not feverish emotionalism. Each term is quite plain and human, and each has equal importance as an attribute of heavenly life. How many politicians—the people to whom we have confided the control of our national existence—work and will in quiet love? What about industry? Do the masters, or the workers, work and will in quiet love? that is to say with diligence and faithful purpose, without selfish anxiety, without selfish demands and hostilities? What about the hurried, ugly and devitalizing existence of our big towns? Can we honestly say that young people reared in them are likely to acquire this temper of heaven? Yet we have been given the secret, the law of spiritual life; and psychologists would agree that it represents too the most favourable of conditions for a full psychic life, the state in which we have access to all our sources of power.

But man will not achieve this state unless he dwells on the idea of it; and, dwelling on that idea, opening his mind to its suggestions, brings its modes of expression into harmony with his thought about the world of daily life. Our spiritual life to-day, such as it is, tends above all to express itself in social activities. Teacher after teacher comes forward to plume himself on the fact that Christianity is now taking a "social form"; that love of our neighbour is not so much the corollary as the equivalent of the love of God, and so forth. Here I am sure that all can supply themselves with illustrative quotations. Yet is there in this state of things nothing but food for congratulation? Is such a view complete? Is nothing left out? Have we not lost the wonder and poetry of the forest in our diligent cultivation of the economically valuable trees; and shall we ever see life truly until we see it with the poet's eyes? There is so much meritorious working and willing; and so little time left for quiet love. A spiritual fussiness—often a material fussiness too—seems to be taking the place of that inward resort to the fontal sources of our being which is the true religious act, our chance of contact with the Spirit. This compensating beat of the fully lived human life, that whole side of existence resumed in the word contemplation, has been left out. "All the artillery of the world," said John Everard, "were they all discharged together at one clap, could not more deaf the ears of our bodies than the clamourings of desires in the soul deaf its ears, so you see a man must go into the silence, or else he cannot hear God speak."[40] And until we remodel our current conception of the Christian life in such a sense as to give that silence and its revelation their full value, I do not think that we can hope to exhibit the triumphing power of the Spirit in human character and human society. Our whole notion of life at present is such as to set up resistances to its inflow. Yet the inner mood, the consciousness, which makes of the self its channel, are accessible to all, if we would but believe this and act on our belief. "Worship," said William Penn, "is the supreme act of a man's life."[41] And what is worship but a reach-out of the finite spirit towards Infinite Life? Here thought must mend the breach which thought has made: for the root of our trouble consists in the fact that there is a fracture in our conception of God and of our relation with Him. We do not perceive the "hidden unity in the Eternal Being"; the single nature and purpose of that Spirit which brought life forth, and shall lead it to full realization.

Here is our little planet, chiefly occupied, to our view, in rushing round the sun; but perhaps found from another angle to fill quite another part in the cosmic scheme. And on this apparently unimportant speck, wandering among systems of suns, the appearance of life and its slow development and ever-increasing sensitization; the emerging of pain and of pleasure; and presently man with his growing capacity for self-affirmation and self-sacrifice, for rapture and for grief. Love with its unearthly happiness, unmeasured devotion, and limitless pain; all the ecstasy, all the anguish that we extract from the rhythm of life and death. It is much, really, for one little planet to bring to birth. And presently another music, which some—not many perhaps yet, in comparison with its population—are able to hear. The music of a more inward life, a sort of fugue in which the eternal and temporal are mingled; and here and there some, already, who respond to it. Those who hear it would not all agree as to the nature of the melody; but all would agree that it is something different in kind from the rhythm of life and death. And in their surrender to this—to which, as they feel sure, the physical order too is really keeping time—they taste a larger life; more universal, more divine. As Plotinus said, they are looking at the Conductor in the midst; and, keeping time with Him, find the fulfilment both of their striving and of their peace.

---

1. Von Hügel: "Essays and Addresses on the Philosophy of Religion," p. 60.
2. Ennead I, 6. 7.
3. Jacob Boehme: "The Way to Christ," Pt. IV.
4. Op. cit., loc. cit.
5. "One Hundred Poems of Kabir," p. 31.
6. Bernard Bosanquet: "What Religion Is" p. 32.
7. Aug.: Conf. VII, 27.
8. "My vision, becoming more purified, entered deeper and deeper into the ray of that Supernal Light, which in itself is true"—Par. XXXIII, 52.
9. "The Tragic Sense of Life In Men and Peoples," p. 194.
10. T. Upton: "The Bases of Religious Belief," p. 363.
11. Blake: "Jerusalem," Cap. i.
12. Nicholson: "The Divāni Shamsi Tabriz," p. 141.
13. Ennead V. i. 3.
14. Kabir, op. cit., p. 41.
15. "Love, whoso loves thee cannot idle be, so sweet to him to taste thee; but every hour he lives in longing that he may love thee more straitly. For in thee the heart so joyful dwells, that he who feels it not can never say how sweet it is to taste thy savour"—Jacopone da Todi: Lauda 101.
16. Isaiah xl, 29-31.
17. Aug.: Conf. X, 28.
18. "Autobiography of the Maharishi Devendranath Tagore," Cap. 12.
19. "Le Journal Spirituel de Lucie-Christine," p. ii.
20. "Autobiography of Maharishi Devendranath Tagore," Cap. 20.
21. Ruysbroeck: "The Book of the XII Béguines;" Cap. 8.
22. Overton: "Life of Wesley." Cap. 2.
23. R.A. Nicholson: "Studies In Islamic Mysticism," Cap. I.
24. "Donne's Sermons," edited by L. Pearsall Smith, p. 236.
25. Ruysbroeck, "The Sparkling Stone," Cap. 14.
26. Bishr-i-Yasin, cf. Nicholson, op. cit., loc. cit.
27. Ennead VI. 9. 4.
28. "Revelations of Divine Love," Cap. II.
29. Pratt: "The Religious Consciousness," Cap. 2.
30. Höffding: "Philosophy of Religion," Pt. II, A
31. Op. cit., Bk. 4, Cap. 1.

32. "Summa contra Gentiles," L. III. Cap. 37.
33. Aug: Conf. VII, 10.
34. "The Liberal and Mystical Writings of William Law," p. 154.
35. Cf. Haldane, "The Reign of Relativity," Cap. VI.
36. Von Hügel: "Eternal Life," p. 385.
37. Ennead I. 4. 6.
38. Boehme: "The Way to Christ," Pt. IV.
39. Blake: "Jerusalem": To the Christians.
40. "Some Gospel Treasures Opened," p. 600.
41. William Penn, "No Cross, No Crown."

CHAPTER II

HISTORY AND THE LIFE OF THE SPIRIT

We have already agreed that, if we wish to grasp the real character of spiritual life, we must avoid the temptation to look at it as merely a historical subject. If it is what it claims to be, it is a form of eternal life, as constant, as accessible to us here and now, as in any so-called age of faith: therefore of actual and present importance, or else nothing at all. This is why I think that the approach to it through philosophy and psychology is so much to be preferred to the approach through pure history. Yet there is a sense in which we must not neglect such history; for here, if we try to enter by sympathy into the past, we can see the life of the Spirit emerging and being lived in all degrees of perfection and under many different forms. Here, through and behind the immense diversity of temperaments which it has transfigured, we can best realise its uniform and enduring character; and therefore our own possibility of attaining to it, and the way that we must tread so to do. History does not exhort us or explain to us, but exhibits living specimens to us; and these specimens witness again and again to the fact that a compelling power does exist in the world—little understood, even by those who are inspired by it—which presses men to transcend their material limitations and mental conflicts, and live a new creative life of harmony, freedom and joy. Directly human character emerges as one of man's prime interests, this possibility emerges too, and is never lost sight of again. Hindu, Buddhist, Egyptian, Greek, Alexandrian, Moslem and Christian all declare with more or less completeness a way of life, a path, a curve of development which shall end in its attainment; and history brings us face to face with the real and human men and women who have followed this way, and found its promise to be true.

It is, indeed, of supreme importance to us that these men and women did truly and actually thus grow, suffer and attain: did so feel the pressure of a more intense life, and the demand of a more authentic love. Their adventures, whatsoever addition legend may have made to them, belong at bottom to the realm of fact, of realistic happening, not of phantasy: and therefore speak not merely to our imagination but to our will. Unless the spiritual life were thus a part of history, it could only have for us the interest of a noble dream: an interest actually less than that of great poetry, for this has at least been given to us by man's hard passionate work of expressing in concrete image—and ever the more concrete, the greater his art—the results of his transcendental contacts with Beauty, Power or Love. Thus, as the tracking-out of a concrete life, a Man, from Nazareth to Calvary, made of Christianity a veritable human revelation of God and not a Gnostic answer to the riddle of the soul; so the real and solid men and women of the Spirit—eating, drinking, working, suffering, loving, each in the circumstances of their own time—are the earnests of our own latent destiny and powers, the ability of the Christian to "grow taller in Christ."[1] These powers—that ability—are factually present in the race, and are totally independent of the specific religious system which may best awaken, nourish, and cause them to grow.

In order, then, that we may be from the first clear of all suspicion of vague romancing about indefinite types of perfection and keep tight hold on concrete life, let us try to re-enter history, and look at the quality of life exhibited by some of these great examples of dynamic spirituality, and the movements which they initiated. It is true that we can only select from among them, but we will try to keep to those who have followed on highest levels a normal course; the upstanding types, varying much in temperament but little in aim and achievement, of that form of life which is re-made and controlled by the Spirit, entinctured with Eternal Life. If such a use of history is indeed to be educative for us, we must avoid the conventional view of it, as a mere chronicle of past events; and of historic personalities as stuffed specimens exhibited against a flat tapestried background, more or less picturesque, but always thought of in opposition to the concrete thickness of the modern world. We are not to think of spiritual epochs now closed; of ages of faith utterly separated from us; of saints

THE LIFE OF THE SPIRIT AND THE LIFE OF TO-DAY

as some peculiar species, God's pet animals, living in an incense-laden atmosphere and less vividly human and various than ourselves. Such conceptions are empty of historical content in the philosophic sense; and when we are dealing with the accredited heroes of the Spirit—that is to say, with the Saints—they are particularly common and particularly poisonous. As Benedetto Croce has observed, the very condition of the existence of real history is that the deed celebrated must live and be present in the soul of the historian; must be emotionally realized by him *now*, as a concrete fact weighted with significance. It must answer to a present, not to a past interest of the race, for thus alone can it convey to us some knowledge of its inward truth.

Consider from this point of view the case of Richard Rolle, who has been called the father of English mysticism. It is easy enough for those who regard spiritual history as dead chronicle and its subjects as something different from ourselves, to look upon Rolle's threefold experience of the soul's reaction to God—the heat of his quick love, the sweetness of his spiritual intercourse, the joyous melody with which it filled his austere, self-giving life[2]—as the probable result of the reaction of a neurotic temperament to mediæval traditions. But if, for instance the Oxford undergraduate of to-day realizes Rolle, not as a picturesque fourteenth-century hermit, but as a fellow-student—another Oxford undergraduate, separated from him only by an interval of time—who gave up that university and the career it could offer him, under the compulsion of another Wisdom and another Love, then he re-enters the living past. If, standing by him in that small hut in the Yorkshire wolds, from which the urgent message of new life spread through the north of England, he hears Rolle saying "Nought more profitable, nought merrier than grace of contemplation, the which lifteth us from low things and presenteth us to God. What thing is grace but beginning of joy? And what is perfection of joy but grace complete?"[3] —if, I say, he so re-enters history that he can hear this as Rolle meant it, not as a poetic phrase but as a living fact, indeed life's very secret—then, his heart may be touched and he may begin to understand. And then it may occur to him that this ardour, and the sacrifice it impelled, the hard life which it supported, witness to another level of being; reprove his own languor and comfort, his contentment with a merely physical mental life, and are not wholly to be accounted for in terms of superstition or of pathology.

When the living spirit in us thus meets the living spirit of the past, our time-span is enlarged, and history is born and becomes contemporary; thus both widening and deepening our vital experience. It then becomes not only a real mode of life to us; but more than this, a mode of social life. Indeed, we can hardly hope without this re-entrance into the time stream to achieve by ourselves, and in defiance of tradition, a true integration of existence. Thus to defy tradition is to refuse all the gifts the past can make to us, and cut ourselves off from the cumulative experiences of the race. The Spirit, as Croce[4] reminds us, is history, makes history, and is also itself the living result of all preceding history; since Becoming is the essential reality, the creative formula, of that life in which we find ourselves immersed.

It is from such an angle as this that I wish to approach the historical aspect of the life of Spirit; re-entering the past by sympathetic imagination, refusing to be misled by superficial characteristics, but seeking the concrete factors of the regenerate life, the features which persist and have significance for it—getting, if we can, face to face with those intensely living men and women who have manifested it. This is not easy. In studying all such experience, we have to remember that the men and women of the Spirit are members of two orders. They have attachments both to time and to eternity. Their characteristic experiences indeed are non-temporal, but their feet are on the earth; the earth of their own day. Therefore two factors will inevitably appear in those experiences, one due to tradition, the other to the free movements of creative life: and we, if we would understand, must discriminate between them. In this power of taking from the past and pushing on to the future, the balance maintained between stability and novelty, we find one of their abiding characteristics. When this balance is broken—when there is either too complete a submission to tradition and authority, or too violent a rejection of it—full greatness is not achieved.

In complete lives, the two things overlap: and so perfectly that no sharp distinction is made between the gifts of authority and of fresh experience. Traditional formulæ, as we all know, are often used because they are found to tally with life, to light up dark corners of our own spirits and give names to experiences which we want to define. Ceremonial deeds are used to actualize free contacts with Reality. And we need not be surprised that they can do this; since tradition represents the crystallization, and handling on under symbols, of all the spiritual experiences of the race.

Therefore the man or woman of the Spirit will always accept and use some tradition; and unless he does so, he is not of much use to his fellow-men. He must not, then, be discredited on account of the symbolic system he adopts; but must be allowed to tell his news in his own way. We must not refuse to find reality within the Hindu's account of his joyous life-giving communion with Ram, any more than we refuse to find it within the Christian's description of his personal converse with Christ. We must not discredit the assurance which comes to the devout Buddhist who faithfully follows the Middle Way, or deny that Pagan sacramentalism was to its initiates a channel of grace. For all these are children of tradition, occupy a given place in the stream of history; and commonly they are better, not worse, for accepting this fact with all that it involves. And on the other hand, as we shall see when we come to discuss the laws of suggestion and the function of belief, the weight of tradition presses the loyal and humble soul which accepts it, to such an interpretation of its own spiritual intuitions as its Church, its creed, its environment give to it. Thus St. Catherine of Genoa, St. Teresa, even Ruysbroeck, are able to describe their intuitive communion with God in strictly Catholic terms; and by so doing renew, enrich and explicate the content of those terms for those who follow them. Those who could not harmonize their own vision of reality with the current formulæ—Fox, Wesley or Blake, driven into opposition by the sterility of the contemporary Church—were forced to find elsewhere some tradition through which to maintain contact with the past. Fox found it in the Bible; Wesley in patristic Christianity. Even Blake's prophetic system, when closely examined, is found to have many historic and Christian connections. And all these regarded themselves far less as bringers-in of novelty, than as restorers of lost truth. So we must be prepared to discriminate the element of novelty from the element of stability; the reality of the intuition, the curve of growth, the moral situation, from the traditional and often symbolic language in which it is given to us. The comparative method helps us towards this; and is thus not, as some would pretend, the servant of scepticism, but rightly used the revealer of the Spirit of Life in its variety of gifts. In this connection we might remember that time—like space—is only of secondary importance to us. Compared with the eons of preparation, the millions of years of our animal and sub-human existence, the life of the Spirit as it appears in human history might well be regarded as simultaneous rather than successive. We may borrow the imagery of Donne's great discourse on Eternity and say, that those heroic livers of the spiritual life whom we idly class in comparison with ourselves as antique, or mediæval men, were "but as a bed of flowers some gathered at six, some at seven, some at eight—all in one morning in respect of this day."[5]

Such a view brings them more near to us, helps us to neglect mere differences of language and appearance, and grasp the warmly living and contemporary character of all historic truth. It preserves us, too, from the common error of discriminating between so-called "ages of faith" and our own. The more we study the past, the more clearly we recognize that there are no "ages of faith." Such labels merely represent the arbitrary cuts which we make in the time-stream, the arbitrary colours which we give to it. The spiritual man or woman is always fundamentally the same kind of man or woman; always reaching out with the same faith and love towards the heart of the same universe, though telling that faith and love in various tongues. He is far less the child of his time, than the transformer of it. His this-world business is to bring in novelty, new reality, fresh life. Yet, coming to fulfil not to destroy, he uses for this purpose the traditions, creeds, even the institutions of his day. But when he has done with them, they do not look the same as they did before. Christ himself has been well called a Constructive Revolutionary,[6] yet each single element of His teaching can be found in Jewish tradition; and the noblest of His followers have the same character. Thus St. Francis of Assisi only sought consistently to apply the teaching of the New Testament, and St. Teresa that of the Carmelite Rule. Every element of Wesleyanism is to be found in primitive Christianity; and Wesleyanism is itself the tradition from which the new vigour of the Salvation Army sprang. The great regenerators of history are always in fundamental opposition to the common life of their day, for they demand by their very existence a return to first principles, a revolution in the ways of thinking and of acting common among men, a heroic consistency and single-mindedness: but they can use for their own fresh constructions and contacts with Eternal Life the material which this life offers to them. The experiments of St. Benedict, St. Francis, Fox or Wesley, were not therefore the natural products of ages of faith. They each represented the revolt of a heroic soul against surrounding apathy and decadence; an invasion of novelty; a sharp break with society, a new use of antique tradition depending on new contacts with the Spirit. Greatness is seldom in harmony with its own epoch, and spiritual greatness least of all. It is usually startlingly modern, even eccentric at the time at which it appears. We are accustomed to think of "The Imitation of Christ" as the classic expression of mediæval spirituality. But when Thomas à Kempis wrote his book, it was the manifesto of that which was called the Modern Devotion; and represented a new attempt to live the life of the Spirit, in opposition to surrounding apathy.

When we re-enter the past, what we find, there is the persistent conflict between this novelty and this apathy; that is to say between man's instinct for transcendence, in which we discern the pressure of the Spirit and the earnest of his future, and his tendency to lag behind towards animal levels, in which we see the influence of his racial past. So far as the individual is concerned, all that religion means by grace is resumed under the first head, much that it means by sin under the second head. And the most striking—though not the only—examples of the forward reach of life towards freedom (that is, of conquering grace) are those persons whom we call men and women of the Spirit. In them it is incarnate, and through them, as it were, it spreads and gives the race a lift: for their transfiguration is never for themselves alone, they impart it to all who follow them. But the downward falling movement ever dogs the emerging life of spirit; and tends to drag back to the average level the group these have vivified, when their influence is withdrawn. Hence the history of the Spirit—and, incidentally, the history of all churches—exhibits to us a series of strong movements towards completed life, inspired by vigorous and transcendent personalities; thwarted by the common indolence and tendency to mechanization, but perpetually renewed. We have no reason to suppose that this history is a closed book, or that the spiritual life struggling to emerge among ourselves will follow other laws.

We desire then, if we can, to discover what it was that these transcendent personalities possessed. We may think, from the point at which we now stand, that they had some things which were false, or, at least, were misinterpreted by them. We cannot without insincerity make their view of the universe our own. But, plainly, they also possessed truths and values which most of us have not: they obtained from their religion, whether we allow that it had as creed an absolute or a symbolic value, a power of living, a courage and clear vision, which we do not as a rule obtain. When we study the character and works of these men and women, observing their nobility, their sweetness, their power of endurance, their outflowing love, we must, unless we be utterly insensitive, perceive ourselves to be confronted by a quality of being which we do not possess. And when we are so fortunate as to meet one of them in the flesh, though his conduct is commonly more normal than our own, we know then with Plotinus that the soul *has* another life. Yet many of us accept the same creedal forms, use the same liturgies, acknowledge the same scale of values and same moral law. But as something, beyond what the ordinary man calls beauty rushes out to the great artist from the visible world, and he at this encounter becomes more vividly alive; so for these there was and is in religion a new, intenser life which they can reach. They seem to represent favourable variations, genuine movements of man towards new levels; a type of life and of greatness, which remains among the hoarded possibilities of the race.

Now the main questions which we have to ask of history fall into two groups:

- First, *Type*. What are the characters which mark this life of the Spirit?
- Secondly, *Process*. What is the line of development by which the individual comes to acquire and exhibit these characters?

First, then, the *Spiritual Type*.

What we see above all in these men and women, so frequently repeated that we may regard it as classic, is a perpetual serious heroic effort to integrate life about its highest factors. Their central quality and real source of power is this single-mindedness. They aim at God: the phrase is Ruysbroeck's, but it pervades the real literature of the Spirit. Thus it is the first principle of Hinduism that "the householder must keep touch with Brahma in all his actions."[7] Thus the Sufi says he has but two laws—to look in one direction and to live in one way.[8] Christians call this, and with reason, the Imitation of Christ; and it was in order to carry forward this imitation more perfectly that all the great Christian systems of spiritual training were framed. The New Testament leaves us in no doubt that the central fact of Our Lord's life was His abiding sense of direct connection with and responsibility to the Father; that His teaching and works of charity alike were inspired by this union; and that He declared it, not as a unique fact, but as a possible human ideal. This Is not a theological, but a historical statement, which applies, in its degree to every man and woman who has been a follower of Christ: for He was, as St. Paul has said, "the eldest in a vast family of brothers." The same single-minded effort and attainment meet us in other great faiths; though these may lack a historic ideal of perfect holiness and love. And by a paradox repeated again and again in human history, it is this utter devotion to the spiritual and eternal which is seen to bring forth the most abundant fruits in the temporal sphere; giving not only the strength to do difficult things, but that creative charity which "wins and redeems the unlovely by the power of its love."[9] The man or woman of prayer, the community devoted to it, tap some deep source of power and use it in the most practical ways. Thus, the only object of the Benedictine rule was the fostering of goodness in those who adopted it, the education of the soul; and it became one of the chief instruments in the civilization of Europe, carrying forward not only religion, but education, pure scholarship, art, and industrial reform. The object of St. Bernard's reform was the restoration of the life of prayer. His monks, going out into the waste places with no provision but their own faith, hope and charity, revived agriculture, established industry, literally compelled the wilderness to flower for God. The Brothers of the Common Life joined together, in order that, living simply and by their own industry, they might observe a rule of constant prayer: and they became in consequence a powerful educational influence. The object of Wesley and his first companions was by declaration the saving of their own souls and the living only to the glory of God; but they were impelled at once by this to practical deeds of mercy, and ultimately became the regenerators of religion in the English-speaking world.

It is well to emphasize this truth, for it conveys a lesson which we can learn from history at the present time with much profit to ourselves. It means that reconstruction of character and reorientation of attention must precede reconstruction of society; that the Sufi is right when he declares that the whole secret lies in looking in one direction and living in one way. Again and again it has been proved, that those who aim at God do better work than those who start with the declared intention of benefiting their fellow-men. We must *be* good before we can *do* good; be real before we can accomplish real things. No generalized benevolence, no social Christianity, however beautiful and devoted, can take the place of this centring of the spirit on eternal values; this humble, deliberate recourse to Reality. To suppose that it can do so, is to fly in the face of history and mistake effect for cause.

This brings us to the *Second Character*: the rich completeness of the spiritual life, the way in which it fuses and transfigures the complementary human tendencies to contemplation and action, the non-successive and successive aspects of reality. "The love of God," said Ruysbroeck, "is an indrawing *and* outpouring tide";[10] and history endorses this. In its greatest representatives, the rhythm of adoration and work is seen in an accentuated form. These people seldom or never answer to the popular idea of idle contemplatives. They do not withdraw from the stream of natural life and effort, but plunge into it more deeply, seek its heart. They have powers of expression and creation, and use them to the full. St. Paul, St. Benedict, St.

Bernard, St. Francis, St. Teresa, St. Ignatius organizing families which shall incarnate the gift of new life; Fox, Wesley and Booth striving to save other men; Mary Slessor driven by vocation from the Dundee mill to the African swamps—these are characteristic of them. We perceive that they are not specialists, as more earthly types of efficiency are apt to be. Theirs are rich natures, their touch on existence has often an artistic quality, St. Paul in his correspondence could break into poetry, as the only way of telling the truth. St. Jerome lived to the full the lives of scholar and of ascetic. St. Francis, in his perpetual missionary activities, still found time for his music songs; St. Hildegarde and St. Catherine of Siena had their strong political interests; Jacopone da Todi combined the careers of contemplative politician and poet. So too in practical matters. St. Catherine of Genoa was one of the first hospital administrators, St. Vincent de Paul a genius in the sphere of organized charity, Elizabeth Fry in that of prison reform. Brother Laurence assures us that he did his cooking the better for doing it in the Presence of God. Jacob Boehme was a hard-working cobbler, and afterwards as a writer showed amazing powers of composition. The perpetual journeyings and activities of Wesley reproduced in smaller compass the career of St. Paul: he was also an exact scholar and a practical educationist. Mary Slessor showed the quality of a ruler as well as that of a winner of souls. In the intellectual region, Richard of St. Victor was supreme in contemplation, and also a psychologist far in advance of his time. We are apt to forget the mystical side of Aquinas; who was poet and contemplative as well as scholastic philosopher.

And the third feature we notice about these men and women is, that this new power by which they lived was, as Ruysbroeck calls it, "a spreading light."[11] It poured out of them, invading and illuminating other men: so that, through them, whole groups or societies were re-born, if only for a time, on to fresh levels of reality, goodness and power. Their own intense personal experience was valid not only for themselves. They belonged to that class of natural, leaders who are capable,—of infecting the herd with their own ideals; leading it to new feeding grounds, improving the common level It is indeed the main social function of the man or woman of the Spirit to be such a crowd-compeller In the highest sense; and, as the artist reveals new beauty to his fellow-men, to stimulate in their neighbours the latent human capacity for God. In every great surge forward to new life, we can trace back the radiance to such a single point of light; the transfiguration of an individual soul. Thus Christ's communion with His Father was the life-centre, the point of contact with Eternity, whence radiated the joy and power of the primitive Christian flock: the classic example of a corporate spiritual life. When the young man with great possessions asked Jesus, "What shall I do to be saved?" Jesus replied in effect, "Put aside all lesser interests, strip off unrealities, and come, give yourself the chance of catching the Infection of holiness from Me." Whatever be our view of Christian dogma, whatever meaning we attach to the words "redemption" and "atonement," we shall hardly deny that in the life and character of the historic Christ something new was thus evoked from, and added to, humanity. No one can read with attention the Gospel and the story of the primitive Church, without being struck by the consciousness of renovation, of enhancement, experienced by all who received the Christian secret in its charismatic stage. This new factor is sometimes called rebirth, sometimes grace, sometimes the power of the Spirit, sometimes being "in Christ." We misread history if we regard it either as a mere gust of emotional fervour, or a theological idea, or discount the "miracles of healing" and other proofs of enhanced power by which it was expressed. Everything goes to prove that the "more abundant life" offered by the Johannine Christ to His followers, was literally experienced by them; and was the source of their joy, their enthusiasm, their mutual love and power of endurance.

On lower levels, and through the inspiration of lesser teachers, history shows us the phenomena of primitive Christianity repeated again and again; both within and without the Christian circle of ideas. Every religion looks for, and most have possessed, some revealer of the Spirit; some Prophet, Buddha, Mahdi, or Messiah. In all, the characteristic demonstrations of the human power of transcendence—a supernatural life which can be lived by us—have begun in one person, who has become a creative centre mediating new life to his fellow-men: as were Buddha and Mohammed for the faiths which they founded. Such lives as those of St. Paul, St. Benedict, St. Francis, Fox, Wesley, Booth are outstanding examples of the operation of this law. The parable of the leaven is in fact an exact description of the way in which the spiritual consciousness—the supernatural urge—is observed to spread in human society. It is characteristic of the regenerate type, that he should as it were overflow his own boundaries and energize other souls: for the gift of a real and harmonized life pours out inevitably from those who possess it to other men. We notice that the great mystics recognize again and again such a fertilizing and creative power, as a mark of the soul's full vitality. It is not the personal rapture of the spiritual marriage, but rather the "divine fecundity" of one who is a parent of spiritual children; which seems to them the goal of human transcendence, and evidence of a life truly lived on eternal levels, in real union with God. "In the fourth and last degree of love the soul brings forth its children," says Richard of St. Victor.[12] "The last perfection to supervene upon a thing," says Aquinas, "is its becoming the cause of other things."[13] In a word, it is creative. And the spiritual life as we see it in history is thus creative; the cause of other things.

History is full of examples of this law: that the man or woman of the spirit is, fundamentally, a life-giver; and all corporate achievement of the life of the spirit flows from some great apostle or initiator, is the fruit of discipleship. Such corporate achievement is a form of group consciousness, brought into being through the power and attraction of a fully harmonized life, infecting others with its own sharp sense of Divine reality. Poets and artists thus infect in a measure all those who yield to their influence. The active mystic, who is the poet of Eternal Life, does it in a supreme degree. Such a relation of master and disciples is conspicuous in every true spiritual revival; and is the link between the personal and corporate aspects of regeneration. We see it in the little flock that followed Christ, the Little Poor Men who followed Francis, the Friends of Fox, the army of General Booth. Not Christianity alone, but Hindu and Moslem history testify to this necessity. The Hindu who is drawn to the spiritual life must find a *guru* who can not only teach its laws but also give its atmosphere; and must accept his discipline in a spirit of obedience. The Sūfi neophyte is directed to place himself in the hands of his *sheikh* "as a corpse in the hands of the washer"; and all the great saints of Islam have been the inspiring centres of more or less organized groups.

History teaches us, in fact, that God most often educates men through men. We most easily recognize Spirit when it is perceived transfiguring human character, and most easily achieve it by means of sympathetic contagion. Though the new light may flash, as it seems, directly into the soul of the specially gifted or the inspired, this spontaneous outbreaking of novelty is comparatively rare; and even here, careful analysis will generally reveal the extent in which environment, tradition, teaching literary or oral, have prepared the way for it. There is no aptitude so great that it can afford to dispense with human experience and education. Even the noblest of the sons and daughters of God are also the sons and daughters of the race; and are helped by those who go before them. And as regards the generality, not isolated effort but the love and sincerity of the true spiritual teacher—and every man and woman of the Spirit is such a teacher within his own sphere of influence—the unselfconscious trust of the disciple, are the means by which the secret of full life has been handed on. "One loving spirit," said St. Augustine, "sets another on fire"; and expressed in this phrase the law which governs the spiritual history of man. This law finds notable expression in the phenomena of the Religious Order; a type of association, found in more or less perfection in every great religion, which has not received the attention it deserves from students of psychology. If we study the lives of those who founded these Orders—though such a foundation was not always intended by them—we notice one general characteristic: each was an enthusiast, abounding in zest and hope, and became in his lifetime a fount of regeneration, a source of spiritual infection, for those who came under his influence. In each the spiritual world was seen "through a temperament," and so mediated to the disciples; who shared so far as they were able the master's special secret and attitude to life. Thus St. Benedict's sane and generous outlook is crystallized in the Benedictine rule. St. Francis' deep sense of the connection between poverty and freedom gave Franciscan regeneration its peculiar character. The heroisms of the early Jesuit missionaries reflected the strong courageous temper of St. Ignatius. The rich contemplative life of Carmel is a direct inheritance from St. Teresa's mystical experience. The great Orders in their purity were families, inheriting and reproducing the salient qualities of their patriarch; who gave, as a father to his children, life stamped with his own characteristics.

Yet sooner or later after the withdrawal of its founder, the group appears to lose its spontaneous and enthusiastic character. Zest fails. Unless a fresh leader be forthcoming, it inevitably settles down again towards the general level of the herd. Thence it can only be roused by means of "reforms" or "revivals," the arrival of new, vigorous leaders, and the formation of new enthusiastic groups: for the bulk of men as we know them cannot or will not make the costing effort needed for a first-hand participation in eternal life. They want a "crowd-compeller" to lift them above themselves. Thus the history of Christianity is the history of successive spiritual group-formations, and their struggle to survive; from the time when Jesus of Nazareth formed His little flock with the avowed aim of "bringing in the Kingdom of God"—transmuting the mentality of the race, and so giving it more abundant life.

Christians appeal to the continued teaching and compelling power of their Master, the influence and infection of His spirit and atmosphere, as the greatest of the regenerative forces still at work within life: and this is undoubtedly true of those devout spirits able to maintain contact with the eternal world in prayer. The great speech of Serenus de Cressy in "John Inglesant" described once for all the highest type of Christian spirituality.[14] But in practice this link and this influence are too subtle for the mass of men. They must constantly be re-experienced by ardent and consecrated souls; and by them be mediated to fresh groups, formed within or without the institutional frame. Thus in the thirteenth century St. Francis, and in the fourteenth the Friends of God, created a true spiritual society within the Church, by restoring in themselves and their followers the lost consistency between Christian idea and Christian life. In the seventeenth and eighteenth centuries, Fox and Wesley possessed by the same essential vision, broke away from the institution which was no longer supple enough to meet their needs, and formed their fresh groups outside the old herd.

When such creative personalities appear and such groups are founded by them, the phenomena of the spiritual life reappear in their full vigour, and are disseminated. A new vitality, a fresh power of endurance, is seen in all who are drawn within the group and share its mind. This is what St. Paul seems to have meant, when he reminded his converts that they had the mind of Christ. The primitive friars, living under the influence of Francis, did practice the perfect poverty which is also perfect joy. The assured calm and willing sufferings of the early Christians were reproduced in the early Quakers, secure in their possession of the inner light. We know very well the essential characters of this fresh mentality; the power, the enthusiasm, the radiant joy, the indifference to pain and hardship it confers. But we can no more produce it from these raw materials than the chemist's crucible can produce life. The whole experience of St. Francis is implied in the Beatitudes. The secret of Elizabeth Fry is the secret of St. John. The doctrine of General Booth is fully stated by St. Paul. But it was not by referring inquirers to the pages of the New Testament that the first brought men fettered by things to experience the freedom of poverty; the second faced and tamed three hundred Newgate criminals, who seemed at her first visit "like wild beasts"; or the third created armies of the redeemed from the dregs of the London Slums. They did these things by direct personal contagion; and they will be done among us again when the triumphant power of Eternal Spirit is again exhibited, not in ideas but in human character.

I think, then, that history justifies us in regarding the full living of the spiritual life as implying at least these three characters. First, single-mindedness: to mean only God. Second, the full integration of the contemplative and active sides of existence, lifted up, harmonized, and completely consecrated to those interests which the self recognizes as Divine. Third, the power of reproducing this life; incorporating it in a group. Before we go on, we will look at one concrete example which illustrates all these points. This example is that of St. Benedict and the Order which he founded; for in the rounded completeness of his life and system we see what should be the normal life of the Spirit, and its result.

Benedict was born in times not unlike our own, when wars had shaken civilization, the arts of peace were unsettled, religion was at a low ebb. As a young man, he experienced an intense revulsion from the vicious futility of Roman society, fled into the hills, and lived in a cave for three years alone with his thoughts of God. It would be easy to regard him as an eccentric boy: but he was adjusting himself to the real centre of his life. Gradually others who longed for a more real existence joined him, and he divided them into groups of twelve, and settled them in small houses; giving them a time-table by which to live, which should make possible a full and balanced existence of body, mind and soul. Thanks to those years of retreat and preparation, he knew what he wanted and what he ought to do; and they ushered in a long life of intense mental and spiritual activity. His houses were schools, which taught the service of God and the perfecting of the soul as the aims of life. His rule, in which genial human tolerance, gentle courtesy, and a profound understanding of men are not less marked than lofty spirituality, is the classic statement of all that the Christian spiritual life implies and should be.[15]

What, then, is the character of the life which St. Benedict proposed as a remedy for the human failure and disharmony that he saw around him? It was framed, of course, for a celibate community: but it has many permanent features which are unaffected by his limitation. It offers balanced opportunities of development to the body, the mind and the spirit; laying equal emphasis on hard work, study, and prayer. It aims at a robust completeness, not at the production of professional ascetics; indeed, its Rule says little about physical austerities, insists on sufficient food and rest, and countenances no extremes. According to Abbot Butler, St. Benedict's day was divided into three and a half hours for public worship, four and a half for reading and meditation, six and a half for manual work, eight and a half for sleep, and one hour for meals. So that in spite of the time devoted to spiritual and mental interests, the primitive Benedictine did a good day's work and had a good night's rest at the end of it. The work might be anything that wanted doing, so long as the hours of prayer were not infringed. Agriculture, scholarship, education, handicrafts and art have all been done perfectly by St. Benedict's sons, working and willing in quiet love. This is what one of the greatest constructive minds of Christendom regarded as a reasonable way of life; a frame within which the loftiest human faculties could grow, and man's spirit achieve that harmony with God which is its goal. Moreover, this life was to be social. It was in the beginning just the busy useful life of an Italian farm, lived in groups—in monastic families, under the rule and inspiration not of a Master but of an Abbot; a Father who really was the spiritual parent of his monks, and sought to train them in the humility, obedience, self-denial and gentle suppleness of character which are the authentic fruits of the Spirit. This ideal, it seems to me, has something still to say to us; some reproof to administer to our hurried and muddled existence, our confusion of values, our failure to find time for reality. We shall find in it and its creator, if we look, all those marks of the regenerate life of the Spirit which history has shown to us as normal: namely the transcendent aim, the balanced career of action and contemplation, the creative power, and above all the principle of social solidarity and discipleship.

We go on to ask history what it has to tell us on the second point, the process by which the individual normally develops this life of the Spirit, the serial changes it demands; for plainly, to know this is of practical importance to us. The full inwardness of these changes will be considered when we come to the personal aspect of the spiritual life. Now we are only concerned to notice that history tends to establish the constant recurrence of a normal process, recognizable alike in great and small personalities under the various labels which have been given to it, by which the self moves from its usually exclusive correspondence with the temporal order to those full correspondences with reality, that union with God, characteristic of the spiritual life. This life we must believe in some form and degree to be possible for all; but we study it best on heroic levels, for here its moments are best marked and its fullest records survive.

The first moment of this process seems to be, that man falls out of love with life as he has commonly lived it, and the world as he has known it. Dissatisfaction and disillusion possess him; the negative marks of his nascent intuition of another life, for which he is intended but which he has not yet found. We see this initial phase very well in St. Benedict, disgusted by the meaningless life of Roman society; in St. Francis, abandoning his gay and successful social existence; in Richard Rolle, turning suddenly from scholarship to a hermit's life; in the restless misery of St. Catherine of Genoa; in Fox, desperately seeking "something that could speak to his condition"; and also in two outstanding examples from modern India, those of the Maharishi Devendranath Tagore and the Sadhu Sundar Singh. This dissatisfaction, sometimes associated with the negative vision or conviction of sin, sometimes with the positive longing for holiness and peace, is the mental preparation of conversion; which, though not a constant, is at least a characteristic feature of the beginning of the spiritual life as seen in history. We might, indeed, expect some crucial change of attitude, some inner crisis, to mark the beginning of a new life which is to aim only at God. Here too we find one motive of that movement of world-abandonment which so commonly follows conversion, especially in heroic souls. Thus St. Paul hides himself in Arabia; St. Benedict retires for three years to the cave at Subiaco; St. Ignatius to Manresa. Gerard Groot, the brilliant and wealthy young Dutchman who founded the brotherhood of the Common Life, began his new life by self-seclusion in a Carthusian cell. St. Catherine of Siena at first lived solitary in her own room. St. Francis with dramatic completeness abandoned his whole past, even the clothing that was part of it. Jacopone da Todi, the prosperous lawyer converted to Christ's poverty, resorted to the most grotesque devices to express his utter separation from the world. Others, it is true, have chosen quieter methods, and found in that which St. Catherine calls the cell of self-knowledge the solitude they required; but *some* decisive break was imperative for all. History assures us that there is no easy sliding into the life of the Spirit.

A secondary cause of such world refusal is the first awakening of the contemplative powers; the intuition of Eternity, hitherto dormant, and felt at this stage to be—in its overwhelming reality and appeal—in conflict with the unreal world and unsublimated active life. This is the controlling idea of the hermit and recluse. It is well seen in St. Teresa; whom her biographers describe as torn, for years, between the interests of human intercourse and the imperative inner voice urging her to solitary self-discipline and prayer. So we may say that in the beginning of the life of the Spirit, as history shows it to us, if disillusion marks the first moment, some measure of asceticism, of world-refusal and painful self-schooling, is likely to mark the second moment.

What we are watching is the complete reconstruction of personality; a personality that has generally grown into the wrong shape. This is likely to be a hard and painful business; and indeed history assures us that it is, and further that the spiritual life is never achieved by taking the line of least resistance and basking in the divine light. With world-refusal, then, is intimately connected stern moral conflict; often lasting for years, and having as its object the conquest of selfhood in all its insidious forms. "Take one step out of yourself," say the Sūfis, "and you will arrive at God."[16] This one step is the most difficult act of life; yet urged by love, man has taken it again and again. This phase is so familiar to every reader of spiritual biography, that I need not insist upon it. "In the field of this body," says Kabir, "a great war goes forward, against passion, anger, pride and greed. It is in the Kingdom of Truth, Contentment and Purity that this battle is raging, and the sword that rings forth most loudly is the sword of His Name."[17] "Man," says Boehme, "must here be at war with himself if he wishes to be a heavenly citizen ... fighting must be the watchword, not with tongue and sword, but with mind and spirit; and not to give over."[18] The need of such a conflict, shown to us in history, is explained on human levels by psychology. On spiritual levels it is made plain to all whose hearts are touched by the love of God. By this way all must pass who achieve the life of the Spirit; subduing to its purposes their wayward wills, and sublimating in its power their conflicting animal impulses. This long effort brings, as its reward a unification of character, an inflow of power: from it we see the mature man or woman of the Spirit emerge. In St. Catherine of Genoa this conflict lasted for four years, after which the thought of sin ceased to rule her consciousness.[19] St. Teresa's intermittent struggles are said to have continued for thirty years. John Wesley, always deeply religious, did not attain the inner stability he calls assurance till he was thirty-five years old. Blake was for twenty years in mental conflict, shut off from the sources of his spiritual life. So slowly do great personalities come to their full stature, and subdue their vigorous impulses to the one ruling idea.

The ending of this conflict, the self's unification and establishment in the new life, commonly means a return more or less complete to that world from which the convert had retreated; taking up of the fully energized and fully consecrated human existence, which must express itself in work no less than in prayer; an exhibition too of the capacity for leadership which is the mark of the regenerate mind. Thus the "first return" of the Buddhist saint is "from the absolute world to the world of phenomena to save all sentient beings."[20] Thus St. Benedict's and St. Catherine of Siena's three solitary years are the preparation for their great and active life works. St. Catherine of Genoa, first a disappointed and world-weary

THE LIFE OF THE SPIRIT AND THE LIFE OF TO-DAY

woman and then a penitent, emerges as a busy and devoted hospital matron and inspired teacher of a group of disciples. St. Teresa's long interior struggles precede her vigorous career as founder and reformer; her creation of spiritual families, new centres of contemplative life. The vast activities of Fox and Wesley were the fruits first of inner conflict, then of assurance—the experience of God and of the self's relation to Him. And on the highest levels of the spiritual life as history shows them to us, this experience and realization, first of profound harmony with Eternity and its interests, next of a personal relation of love, last of an indwelling creative power, a givenness, an energizing grace, reaches that completeness to which has been given the name of union with God.

The great man or woman of the Spirit who achieves this perfect development is, it is true, a special product: a genius, comparable with great creative personalities in other walks of life. But he neither invalidates the smaller talent nor the more general tendency in which his supreme gift takes its rise. Where he appears, that tendency is vigorously stimulated. Like other artists, he founds a school; the spiritual life flames up, and spreads to those within his circle of influence. Through him, ordinary men, whose aptitude for God might have remained latent, obtain a fresh start; an impetus to growth. There is a sense in which he might say with the Johannine Christ, "He that receiveth me receiveth Him that sent me"; for yielding to his magnetism, men really yield to the drawing of the Spirit itself. And when they do this, their lives are found to reproduce—though with less intensity—the life history of their leader. Therefore the main characters of that life history, that steady undivided process of sublimation; are normal human characters. We too may heal the discords of our moral nature, learn to judge existence in the universal light, bring into consciousness our latent transcendental sense, and keep ourselves so spiritually supple that alike in times of stress and hours of prayer and silence we are aware of the mysterious and energizing contact of God. Psychology suggests to us that the great spiritual personalities revealed in history are but supreme instances of a searching self-adjustment and of a way of life, always accessible to love and courage, which all men may in some sense undertake.

---

1. Everard, "Some Gospel Treasures Opened," p. 555
2. *Canor Dulcor, Canor;* cf. Rolle: "The Fire of Love," Bk. 1, Cap. 14
3. Rolle: "The Mending of Life," Cap. XII.

4. Benedetto Croce: "Theory and History of Historiography," trans. by Douglas Ainslie, p. 25.
5. "Donne's Sermons," p. 236.
6. B.H. Streeter, in "The Spirit," p. 349 *seq*.
7. "Autobiography of Maharishi Devendranath Tagore," Cap. 23.
8. R.A. Nicholson: "Studies in Islamic Mysticism," Cap. i.
9. Baron von Hügel In the "Hibbert Journal," July, 1921.
10. Ruysbroeck: "The Sparkling Stone," Cap. 10.
11. Ruysbroeck: "The Adornment of the Spiritual Marriage," Bk. II, Cap. 39.
12. R. of St. Victor: "De Quatuor Gradibus Violentæ Charitatis" (Migne, Pat. Lat.) T. 196, Col. 1216.
13. "Summa Contra Gentiles," Bk. III, Cap. 21.
14. J.E. Shorthouse: "John Inglesant," Cap. 19.
15. Cf. Delatte: "The Rule of St. Benedict"; and C. Butler: "Benedictine Monachism.
16. R.A. Nicholson: "Studies in Islamic Mysticism," Cap. 1.
17. "One Hundred Poems of Kabir," p. 44.
18. Boehme: "Six Theosophic Points," p. 111.
19. Cf. Von Hügel: "The Mystical Element of Religion," Vol. I, Pt. II.
20. McGovern: "An Introduction to Mahāyāna Buddhism," p. 175.

CHAPTER III

PSYCHOLOGY AND THE LIFE OF THE SPIRIT
(I) THE ANALYSIS OF MIND

Having interrogated history in our attempt to discover the essential character of the life of the Spirit, wherever it is found, we are now to see what psychology has to tell us or hint to us of its nature; and of the relation in which it stands to the mechanism of our psychic life. It is hardly necessary to say that such an inquiry, fully carried out, would be a life-work. Moreover, it is an inquiry which we are not yet in a position to undertake. True, more and more material is daily becoming available for it: but many of the principles involved are, even yet, obscure. Therefore any conclusions at which we may arrive can only be tentative; and the theories and schematic representations that we shall be obliged to use must be regarded as mere working diagrams—almost certainly of a temporary character—but useful to us, because they do give us an interpretation of inner experience with which we can deal. I need not emphasize the extent in which modern developments of psychology are affecting our conceptions of the spiritual life, and our reading of many religious phenomena on which our ancestors looked with awe. When we have eliminated the more heady exaggerations of the psycho-analysts, and the too-violent simplifications of the behaviourists, it remains true that many problems have lately been elucidated in an unexpected, and some in a helpful, sense. We are learning in particular to see in true proportion those abnormal states of trance and ecstasy which were once regarded as the essentials, but are now recognized as the by-products, of the mystical life.

But a good deal that at first sight seems startling, and even disturbing to the religious mind, turns out on investigation to be no more than the re-labelling of old facts, which behind their new tickets remain unchanged. Perhaps no generation has ever been so much at the mercy of such labels as our own. Thus many people who are inclined to jibe at the doctrine of original sin welcome it with open arms when it is reintroduced as the uprush of primitive instinct. Opportunity of confession to a psychoanalyst is eagerly sought and gladly paid for, by troubled spirits who would never resort for the same purpose to a priest. The formulæ of auto-suggestion are freely used by those who repudiate vocal prayer and acts of faith with scorn. If, then, I use for the purpose of exposition some of those labels which are affected by the newest schools, I do so without any suggestion that they represent the only valid way of dealing with the psychic life of man. Indeed, I regard these labels as little more than exceedingly clever guesses at truth. But since they are now generally current and often suggestive, it is well that we should try to find a place for spiritual experience within the system which they represent; thus carrying through the principle on which we are working, that of interpreting the abiding facts of the spiritual life, so far as we can, in the language of the present day.

First, then, I propose to consider the analysis of mind, and what It has to tell us about the nature of Sin, of Salvation, of Conversion; what light it casts on the process of purgation or self-purification which is demanded by all religions of the Spirit; what are the respective parts played by reason and instinct in the process of regeneration; and the importance for religious experience of the phenomena of apperception.

We need not at this point consider again all that we mean by the life of the Spirit. We have already considered it as it appears in history—its inexhaustible variety, its power, nobility, and grace. We need only to remind ourselves that what we have got to find room for in our psychological scheme is literally, a changed and enhanced life; a life which, immersed in the stream of history, is yet poised on the eternal world. This life involves a complete re-direction of our desires and impulses, a transfiguration of character; and often, too, a sense of subjugation to superior guidance, of an access of impersonal strength, so overwhelming as to give many of its activities an inspirational or automatic character. We found that this life was marked by a rhythmic alternation between receptivity and activity, more complete and purposeful than the rhythm of work and rest which conditions, or should condition, the healthy life of sense. This re-direction and transfiguration, this removal to a higher term of our mental rhythm, are of course psychic phenomena; using this word in a broad sense, without prejudice to the discrimination of any one aspect of it as spiritual. All that we mean at the moment is, that the change which brings in the spiritual life is a change in the mind and heart of man, working in the stuff of our common human nature, and involving all that the modern psychologist means by the word psyche.

We begin therefore with the nature of the psyche as this modern, growing, changing psychology conceives it; for this is the raw material of regenerate man. If we exclude those merely degraded and pathological theories which have resulted from too exclusive a study of degenerate minds, we find that the current conception of the psyche—by which of course I do not mean the classic conceptions of Ward or even William James—was anticipated by Plotinus, when he said in the Fourth Ennead, that every soul has something of the lower life for the purposes of the body and of the higher for the purposes of the Spirit, and yet constitutes a unity; an unbroken series of ascending values and powers of response, from the levels of merely physical and mainly unconscious life to those of the self-determining and creative consciousness.[1] We first discover psychic energy as undifferentiated directive power, controlling response and adaption to environment; and as it develops, ever increasing the complexity of its impulses and habits, yet never abandoning anything of its past. Instinct represents the correspondence of this life-force with mere nature, its effort as it were to keep its footing and accomplish its destiny in the world of time. Spirit represents this same life acting on highest levels, with most vivid purpose; seeking and achieving correspondence with the eternal world, and realities of the loftiest order yet discovered to be accessible to us. We are compelled to use words of this kind; and the proceeding is harmless enough so long as we remember that they are abstractions, and that we have no real reason to suppose breaks in the life process which extends from the infant's first craving for food and shelter to the saint's craving for the knowledge of God. This urgent, craving life is the dominant characteristic of the psyche. Thought is but the last come and least developed of its powers; one among its various responses to environment, and ways of laying hold on experience.

This conception of the multiplicity in unity of the psyche, conscious and unconscious, is probably one of the most important results of recent psychological advance. It means that we cannot any longer in the good old way rule off bits or aspects of it, and call them intellect, soul, spirit, conscience and so forth; or, on the other hand, refer to our "lower" nature as if it were something separate from ourselves. I am spirit when I pray, if I pray rightly. I am my lower nature, when my thoughts and deeds are swayed by my primitive impulses and physical longings, declared or disguised. I am most wholly myself when that impulsive nature and that craving spirit are welded into one, subject to the same emotional stimulus, directed to one goal. When theologians and psychologists, ignoring this unity of the self, set up arbitrary divisions—and both classes are very fond of doing so—they are merely making diagrams for their own convenience. We ourselves shall probably be compelled to do this: and the proceeding is harmless enough, so long as we recollect that these diagrams are at best symbolic pictures of fact. Specially is it necessary to keep our heads, and refuse to be led away by the constant modern talk of the primitive, unconscious, foreconscious instinctive and other minds which are so prominent in modern psychological literature, or by the spatial suggestions of such terms as threshold, complex, channel of discharge: remembering always the central unity and non-material nature of that many-faced psychic life which is described under these various formulæ.

If we accept this central unity with all its implications, it follows that we cannot take our superior and conscious faculties, set them apart, and call them "ourselves"; refusing responsibility for the more animal and less fortunate tendencies and instincts which surge up with such distressing ease and frequency from the deeps, by attributing these to nature or heredity. Indeed, more and more does it become plain that the sophisticated surface-mind which alone we usually recognize is the smallest, the least developed, and in some respects still the least important part of the real self: that whole man of impulse, thought and desire, which it is the business of religion to capture and domesticate for God. That whole man is an animal-spirit, a living, growing, plastic unit; moving towards a racial future yet unperceived by us, and carrying with him a racial past which conditions at every moment his choices, impulses and acts. Only the most rigid self-examination will disclose to us the extent in which the jungle and the Stone Age are still active in our games, our politics and our creeds; how many of our motives are still those of primitive man, and how many of our social institutions offer him a discreet opportunity of self-expression.

Here, as it seems to me, is a point at which the old thoughts of religion and the new thoughts of psychology may unite and complete one another. Here the scientific conception of the psyche is merely restating the fundamental Christian paradox, that man is truly one, a living, growing spirit,

THE LIFE OF THE SPIRIT AND THE LIFE OF TO-DAY

the creature and child of the Divine Life; and yet that there seem to be in him, as it were, two antagonistic natures—that duality which St. Paul calls the old Adam and the new Adam. The law of the flesh and the law of the spirit, the earthward-tending life of mere natural impulse and the quickening life of re-directed desire, the natural and the spiritual man, are conceptions which the new psychologist can hardly reject or despise. True, religion and psychology may offer different rationalizations of the facts. That which one calls original sin, the other calls the instinctive mind: but the situation each puts before us is the same. "I find a law," says St. Paul, "that when I would do good evil is present with me. For I delight in the law of God after the inward man *but* I see another law in my members warring against the law of my mind.... With the mind I myself serve the law of God, but with the flesh the law of sin." Without going so far as a distinguished psychoanalyst who said in my hearing, "If St. Paul had come to me, I feel I could have helped him," I think it is clear that we are learning to give a new content to this, and many other sayings of the New Testament. More and more psychology tends to emphasize the Pauline distinction; demonstrating that the profound disharmony existing in most civilized men between the impulsive and the rational life, the many conflicts which sap his energy, arise from the persistence within us of the archaic and primitive alongside the modern mind. It demonstrates that the many stages and constituents of our psychic past are still active in each one of us; though often below the threshold of consciousness. The blindly instinctive life, with its almost exclusive interests in food, safety and reproduction; the law of the flesh in its simplest form, carried over from our pre-human ancestry and still capable of taking charge when we are off our guard. The more complex life of the human primitive; with its outlook of wonder, self-interest and fear, developed under conditions of ignorance, peril and perpetual struggle for life. The history of primitive man covers millions of years: the history of civilized man, a few thousand at the most. Therefore it is not surprising that the primitive outlook should have bitten hard into the plastic stuff of the developing psyche, and forms still the infantile foundation of our mental life. Finally, there is the rational life, so far as the rational is yet achieved by us; correcting, conflicting with, and seeking to refine and control the vigour of primitive impulse.

But if it is to give an account of all the facts psychology must also point out, and find place for, the last-comer in the evolutionary series: the rare and still rudimentary achievement of the spiritual consciousness, bearing witness that we are the children of God, and pointing, not backward to the roots but onward to the fruits of human growth. But it cannot allow us to think of this spiritual life as something separate from, and wholly unconditioned by, our racial past. We must rather conceive it as the crown of our psychic evolution, the end of that process which began in the dawn of consciousness and which St. Paul calls "growing up into the stature of Christ." Here psychology is in harmony with the teaching of those mystics who invite us to recognize, not a completed spirit, but rather a seed within us. In the spiritual yearnings, the profound and yet uncertain stirrings of the religious consciousness, its half-understood impulses to God, we perceive the floating-up into the conscious field of this deep germinal life. And psychology warns us, I think, that in our efforts to forward the upgrowth of this spiritual life, we must take into account those earlier types of reaction to the universe which still continue underneath our bright modern appearance, and still inevitably condition and explain so many of our motives and our deeds. It warns us that the psychic growth of humanity is slow and uneven; and that every one of us still retains, though not always it is true in a recognizable form, many of the characters of those stages of development through which the race has passed—characters which inevitably give their colour to our religious no less than to our social life.

"I desire," says à Kempis, "to enjoy thee inwardly but I cannot take thee. I desire to cleave to heavenly things but fleshly things and unmortified passions depress me. I will in my mind be above all things but in despite of myself I am constrained to be beneath, so I unhappy man fight with myself and am made grievous to myself while the spirit seeketh what is above and the flesh what is beneath. O what I suffer within while I think on heavenly things in my mind; the company of fleshly things cometh against me when I pray."[2]

"Oh Master," says the Scholar in Boehme's great dialogue, "the creatures that live in me so withhold me, that I cannot wholly yield and give myself up as I willingly would."[3]

No psychologist has come nearer to a statement of the human situation than have these old specialists in the spiritual life.

The bearing of all this on the study of organized religion is of course of great importance; and will be discussed in a subsequent section. All that I wish to point out now is that the beliefs, and the explanations of action, put forward by our rationalizing surface consciousness are often mere veils which drape the crudeness of our real desires and reactions to life; and that before life can be reintegrated about its highest centres, these real beliefs and motives must be tracked down, and their humiliating character acknowledged. The ape and the tiger, in fact, are not dead in any one of us. In polite persons they are caged, which Is a very different thing: and a careful introspection will teach us to recognize their snarls and chatterings, their urgent requests for more mutton chops or bananas, under the many disguises which they assume—disguises which are not infrequently borrowed from ethics or from religion. Thus a primitive desire for revenge often masquerades as justice, and an unedifying interest in personal safety can be discerned in at least some interpretations of atonement, and some aspirations towards immortality.[4]

I now go on to a second point. It will already be clear that the modern conception of the many-levelled psyche gives us a fresh standpoint from which to consider the nature of Sin. It suggests to us, that the essence of much sin is conservatism, or atavism: that it is rooted in the tendency of the instinctive life to go on, in changed circumstances, acting in the same old way. Virtue, perfect rightness of correspondence with our present surroundings, perfect consistency of our deeds with our best ideas, is hard work. It means the sublimation of crude instinct, the steady control of impulse by such reason as we possess; and perpetually forces us to use on new and higher levels that machinery of habit-formation, that power of implanting tendencies in the plastic psyche, to which man owes his earthly dominance. When our unstable psychic life relaxes tension and sinks to lower levels than this, and it Is always tending so to do, we are relapsing to antique methods of response, suitable to an environment which is no longer there. Few people go through life without knowing what it is to feel a sudden, even murderous, impulse to destroy the obstacle in their path; or seize, at all costs, that which they desire. Our ancestors called these uprushes the solicitations of the devil, seeking to destroy the Christian soul; and regarded them with justice as an opportunity of testing our spiritual strength. It is true that every man has within him such a tempting spirit; but its characters can better be studied in the Zoological Gardens than in the convolutions of a theological hell. "External Reason," says Boehme, "supposes that hell is far from us. But it is near us. Every one carries it in himself."[5] Many of our vices, in fact, are simply savage qualities—and some are even savage virtues—in their old age. Thus in an organized society the acquisitiveness and self-assertion proper to a vigorous primitive dependent on his own powers survive as the sins of envy and covetousness, and are seen operating in the dishonesty of the burglar, the greed and egotism of the profiteer: and, on the highest levels, the great spiritual sin of pride may be traced back to a perverted expression of that self-regarding instinct without which the individual could hardly survive.

When therefore qualities which were once useful on their own level are outgrown but unsublimated, and check the movement towards life's spiritualization, then—whatever they may be—they belong to the body of death, not to the body of life, and are "sin." "Call sin a lump—none other thing than thyself," says "The Cloud of Unknowing."[6] Capitulation to it is often brought about by mere slackness, or, as religion would say, by the mortal sin of sloth; which Julian of Norwich declares to be one of the two most deadly sicknesses of the soul. Sometimes; too, sin is deliberately indulged in because of the perverse satisfaction which this yielding to old craving gives us. The violent-tempered man becomes once more a primitive, when he yields to wrath. A starved and repressed side of his nature—the old Adam, in fact—leaps up into consciousness and glories in its strength. He obtains from the explosion an immense feeling of relief; and so too with the other great natural passions which our religious or social morality keeps in check. Even the saints have known these revenges of natural instincts too violently denied. Thoughts of obscene words and gestures came unasked to torment the pure soul of Catherine of Siena.[7] St. Teresa complained that the devil sometimes sent her so offensive a spirit of bad temper that she could eat people up.[8] Games and sport of a combative or destructive kind provide an innocent outlet for a certain amount of this unused ferocity; and indeed the chief function of games in the modern state is to help us avoid occasions of sin. The sinfulness of any deed depends, therefore, on this theory, on the extent in which it involves retrogression from the point we have achieved: failure to correspond with the light we possess. The inequality of the moral standard all over the world is a simple demonstration of this fact: for many a deed which is innocent in New Guinea, would in London provoke the immediate attention of the police.

Does not this view of sin, as primarily a fall-back to past levels of conduct and experience, a defeat of the spirit of the future in its conflict with the undying past, give us a fresh standpoint from which to look at the idea of Salvation? We know that all religions of the spirit have based their claim upon man on such an offer of salvation: on the conviction that there is something from which he needs to be rescued, if he is to achieve a satisfactory life. What is it, then, from which he must be saved?

I think that the answer must be, from conflict: the conflict between the pull-back of his racial origin and the pull-forward of his spiritual destiny, the antagonism between the buried Titan and the emerging soul, each tending towards adaptation to a different order of reality. We may as well acknowledge that man as he stands is mostly full of conflicts and resistances: that the trite verse about "fightings and fears within, without" does really describe the unregenerate yet sensitive mind with its ineffective struggles, its inveterate egotism, its inconsistent impulses and loves. Man's young will and reason need some reinforcement, some helping power, if they are to conquer and control his archaic impulsive life. And this salvation, this extrication from the wrongful and atavistic claims of primitive impulse in its many strange forms, is a prime business of religion; sometimes achieved in the sudden convulsion we call conversion, and sometimes by the slower process of education. The wrong way to do it is seen in the methods of the Puritan and the extreme ascetic, where all animal impulse is regarded as "sin" and repressed: a proceeding which involves the risk of grave physical and mental disorder, and produces even at the best a bloodless pietism. The right way to do it was described once for all by Jacob Boehme, when he said that it was the business of a spiritual man to "harness his fiery energies to the service of the light—" that is to say, change the direction of our passionate cravings for satisfaction, harmonize and devote them to spiritual ends. This is true regeneration: this is the salvation offered to man, the healing of his psychic conflict by the unification of his instinctive and his ideal life. The voice which St. Mechthild heard, saying "Come and be reconciled," expresses the deepest need of civilized but unspiritualized humanity.

This need for the conversion or remaking of the instinctive life, rather than the achievement of mere beliefs, has always been appreciated by real spiritual teachers; who are usually some generations in advance of the psychologists. Here they agree in finding the "root of evil," the heart of the "old man" and best promise of the "new." Here is the raw material both of vice and of virtue—namely, a mass of desires and cravings which are in themselves neither moral nor immoral, but natural and self-regarding. "In will, imagination and desire," says William Law, "consists the life or fiery driving of every intelligent creature."[9] The Divine voice which said to Jacopone da Todi "Set love in order, thou that lovest Me!" declared the one law of mental growth.[10] To use for a moment the language of mystical theology, conversion, or repentance, the first step towards the spiritual life, consists in a change in the direction of these cravings and desires; purgation or purification, in which the work begun in conversion is made complete, in their steadfast setting in order or re-education, and that refinement and fixation of the most desirable among them which we call the formation of habit, and which is the essence of character building. It is from this hard, conscious and deliberate work of adapting our psychic energy to new and higher correspondences, this costly moral effort and true self-conquest, that the spiritual life in man draws its earnestness, reality and worth.

"Oh, Academicus," says William Law, in terms that any psychologist would endorse, "forget your scholarship, give up your art and criticism, be a plain man; and then the first rudiments of sense may teach you that there, and there only, can goodness be, where it comes forth as a birth of Life, and is the free natural work and fruit of that which lives within us. For till goodness thus comes from a Life within us, we have in truth none at all. For reason, with all its doctrine, discipline, and rules, can only help us to be so good, so changed, and amended, as a wild beast may be, that by restraints and methods is taught to put on a sort of tameness, though its wild nature is all the time only restrained, and in a readiness to break forth again as occasion shall offer."[11] Our business, then, is not to restrain, but to put the wild beast to work, and use its mighty energies; for thus only shall we find the power to perform hard acts. See the young Salvation Army convert turning over the lust for drink or sexual satisfaction to the lust to save his fellow-men. This transformation or sublimation is not the work of reason. His instinctive life, the main source of conduct, has been directed into a fresh channel of use.

We may now look a little more closely at the character and potentialties of our instinctive life: for this life is plainly of the highest importance to us, since it will either energize or thwart all the efforts of the rational self. Current psychology, even more plainly than religion, encourages us to recognize in this powerful instinctive nature the real source of our conduct, the origin of all those dynamic personal demands, those impulses to action, which condition the full and successful life of the natural man. Instincts in the animal and the natural man are the methods by which the life force takes care of its own interests, insures its own full development, its unimpeded forward drive. In so far as we form part of the animal kingdom our own safety, property, food, dominance, and the reproduction of our own type, are inevitably the first objects of our instinctive care. Civilized life has disguised some of these crude demands and the behaviour which is inspired by them, but their essential character remains unchanged. Love and hate, fear and wonder, self-assertion and self-abasement, the gregarious, the acquisitive, the constructive tendencies, are all

THE LIFE OF THE SPIRIT AND THE LIFE OF TO-DAY

expressions of instinctive feeling; and can be traced back to our simplest animal needs.

But instincts are not fixed tendencies: they are adaptable. This can be seen clearly in the case of animals whose environment Is artificially changed. In the dog, for instance, loyalty to the interests of the pack has become loyalty to his master's household. In man, too, there has already been obvious modification and sublimation of many instincts. The hunting impulse begins in the jungle, and may end in the philosopher's exploration of the Infinite. It is the combative instinct which drives the reformer headlong against the evils of the world, as it once drove two cave men at each others' throats. Love, which begins in the mergence of two cells, ends in the saint's supreme discovery, "Thou art the Love wherewith the heart loves Thee."[12] The much advertized herd instinct may weld us into a mob at the mercy of unreasoning passions; but it can also make us living members of the Communion of Saints. The appeals of the prophet and the revivalist, the Psalmist's "Taste and see," the Baptist's "Change your hearts," are all invitations to an alteration in the direction of desire, which would turn our instinctive energies in a new direction and begin the domestication of the human soul for God.

This, then, is the real business of conversion and of the character building that succeeds it; the harnessing of instinct to idea and its direction into new and more lofty channels of use, transmuting the turmoil of man's merely egoistic ambitions, anxieties and emotional desires into fresh forms of creative energy, and transferring their interest from narrow and unreal to universal objectives. The seven deadly sins of Christian ethics—Pride, Anger, Envy, Avarice, Sloth, Gluttony, and Lust—represent not so much deliberate wrongfulness, as the outstanding forms of man's uncontrolled and self-regarding instincts; unbridled self-assertion, ruthless acquisitiveness, and undisciplined indulgence of sense. The traditional evangelical virtues of Poverty, Chastity and Obedience which sum up the demands of the spiritual life exactly oppose them. Over against the self-assertion of the proud and angry is set the ideal of humble obedience, with its wise suppleness and abnegation of self-will. Over against the acquisitiveness of the covetous and envious is set the ideal of inward poverty, with its liberation from the narrow self-interest of I, Me and Mine. Over against the sensual indulgence of the greedy, lustful and lazy is set the ideal of chastity, which finds all creatures pure to enjoy, since it sees them in God, and God in all creatures. Yet all this, rightly understood, is no mere policy of repression. It is rather a rational policy of release, freeing for higher activities instinctive force too often thrown away. It is giving the wild beast his work to do, training him. Since the instincts represent the efforts of this urgent life in us to achieve self-protection and self-realization, it is plain that the true regeneration of the psyche, its redirection from lower to higher levels, can never be accomplished without their help. We only rise to the top of our powers when the whole man acts together, urged by an enthusiasm or an instinctive need.

Further, a complete and ungraduated response to stimulus—an "all-or-none reaction"—is characteristic of the instinctive life and of the instinctive life alone. Those whom it rules for the time give themselves wholly to it; and so display a power far beyond that of the critical and the controlled. Thus, fear or rage will often confer abnormal strength and agility. A really dominant instinct is a veritable source of psycho-physical energy, unifying and maintaining in vigour all the activities directed to its fulfilment.[13] A young man in love is stimulated not only to emotional ardour, but also to hard work in the interests of the future home. The explorer develops amazing powers of endurance; the inventor in the ecstasy of creation draws on deep vital forces, and may carry on for long periods without sleep or food. If we apply this law to the great examples of the spiritual life, we see in the vigour and totality of their self-giving to spiritual interests a mark of instinctive action; and in the power, the indifference to hardship which these selves develop, the result of unification, of an "all-or-none" response to the religious or philanthropic stimulus. It helps us to understand the cheerful austerities of the true ascetic; the superhuman achievement of St. Paul, little hindered by the "thorn in the flesh"; the career of St. Joan of Arc; the way in which St. Teresa or St. Ignatius, tormented by ill-health, yet brought their great conceptions to birth; the powers of resistance displayed by George Fox and other Quaker saints. It explains Mary Slessor living and working bare-foot and bare-headed under the tropical sun, disdaining the use of mosquito nets, eating native food, and taking with impunity daily risks fatal to the average European.[14] It shows us, too, why the great heroes of the spiritual life so seldom think out their positions, or husband their powers. They act because they are impelled: often in defiance of all prudent considerations! yet commonly with an amazing success. Thus General Booth has said that he was driven by "the impulses and urgings of an undying ambition" to save souls. What was this impulse and urge? It was the instinctive energy of a great nature in a sublimated form. The level at which this enhanced power is experienced will determine its value for life; but its character is much the same in the convert at a revival, in the postulant's vivid sense of vocation and consequent break with the world? in the disinterested man of science consecrated to the search for truth, and in the apostle's self-giving to the service of God, with its answering gift of new strength and fruitfulness. Its secret, and indeed the secret of all transcendence is implied In the direction of the old English mystic: "Mean God all, all God, so that nought work in thy wit and in thy will, but only God,"[15] The over-belief, the religious formula in which this instinctive passion is expressed, is comparatively unimportant The revivalist, wholly possessed by concrete and anthropomorphic ideas of God which are impossible to a man of different —and, as we suppose, superior—education, can yet, because of the burning reality with which he lives towards the God so strangely conceived, infect those with whom he comes in contact with the spiritual life.

We are now in a position to say that the first necessity of the life of the Spirit is the sublimation of the instinctive life, involving the transfer of our interest and energy to new objectives, the giving of our old vigour to new longings and new loves. It appears that the invitation of religion to a change of heart, rather than a change of belief, is founded on solid psychological laws. I need not dwell on the way in which Divine love, as the saints have understood it, answers to the complete sublimation of our strongest natural passion; or the extent in which the highest experiences of the religious life satisfy man's instinctive craving for self-realization within a greater Reality, how he feels himself to be fed with a mysterious food, quickened by a fresh dower of life, assured of his own safety within a friendly universe, given a new objective for his energy. It is notorious that one of the most striking things about a truly spiritual man is, that he has achieved a certain stability which others lack. In him, the central craving of the psyche for more life and more love has reached its bourne; instead of feeding upon those secondary objects of desire which may lull our restlessness but cannot heal it He loves the thing which he ought to love, wants to do the deeds which he ought to do, and finds all aspects of his personality satisfied in one objective. Every one has really a forced option between the costly effort to achieve this sublimation of impulse, this unification of the self on spiritual levels, and the quiet evasion of it which is really a capitulation to the animal instincts and unordered cravings of our many-levelled being. We cannot stand still; and this steady downward pull keeps us ever in mind of all the backward-tending possibilities collectively to be thought of as sin, and explains to us why sloth, lack of spiritual energy, is held by religion to be one of the capital forms of human wrongness.

I go on to another point, which I regard as of special importance.

It must not be supposed that the life of the Spirit begins and with the sublimation of, the instinctive and emotional life; though this is indeed for it a central necessity. Nor must we take it for granted that the apparent redirection of impulse to spiritual objects is always and inevitably an advance. All who are or may be concerned with the spiritual training, help, and counselling of others ought clearly to recognize that there are elements in religious experience which represent, not a true sublimation, but either disguised primitive cravings and ideas, or uprushes from lower instinctive levels: for these experiences have their special dangers. As we shall see when we come to their more detailed study, devotional practices tend to produce that state which psychologists call mobility of the threshold of consciousness; and may easily permit the emergence of natural inclinations and desires, of which the self does not recognize the real character. As a matter of fact, a good deal of religious emotion is of this kind. Instances are the childish longing for mere protection, for a sort of supersensual petting, the excessive desire for shelter and rest, voiced in too many popular hymns; the subtle form of self-assertion which can be detected in some claims to intercourse with God—e.g. the celebrated conversation of Angela of Foligno with the Holy Ghost;[16] the thinly veiled human feelings which find expression in the personal raptures of a certain type of pious literature, and in what has been well described as the "divine duet" type of devotion. Many, though not all of the supernormal phenomena of mysticism are open to the same suspicion: and the Church's constant insistence on the need of submitting these to some critical test before, accepting them at face value, is based on a most wholesome scepticism. Though a sense of meek dependence on enfolding love and power is the very heart of religion, and no intense spiritual life is possible unless it contain a strong emotional element, it is of first importance to be sure that its affective side represents a true sublimation of human feelings and desires, and not merely an oblique indulgence of lower cravings.

Again, we have to remember that the instinctive self, powerful though it be? does not represent the sum total of human possibility. The maximum of man's strength is not reached until all the self's powers, the instinctive and also the rational, are united and set on one objective; for then only is he safe from the insidious inner conflict between natural craving and conscious purpose which saps his energies, and is welded into a complete and harmonious instrument of life, "The source of power," says Dr. Hadfield in "The Spirit," "lies not in instinctive emotion alone, but in instinctive emotion expressed in a way with which the whole man can, for the time being at least, identify himself. Ultimately, this is impossible without the achievement of a harmony of all the instincts *and* the approval of the reason."[17]

Thus we see that any unresolved conflict or divorce between the religious instinct and the intellect will mar the full power of the spiritual life: and that an essential part of the self's readjustment to reality must consist in the uniting of these partners, as intellect and intuition are united in creative art. The noblest music, most satisfying poetry are neither the casual results of uncriticized inspiration nor the deliberate fabrications of the brain, but are born of the perfect fusion of feeling and of thought; for the greatest and most fruitful minds are those which are rich and active on both levels—which are perpetually raising blind impulse to the level of conscious purpose, uniting energy with skill, and thus obtaining the fiery energies of the instinctive life for the highest uses. So too the spiritual life is only seen in its full worth and splendour when the whole man is subdued to it, and one object satisfies the utmost desires of heart and mind. The spiritual impulse must not be allowed to become the centre of a group of specialized feelings, a devotional complex, in opposition to, or at least alienated from, the intellectual and economic life. It must on the contrary brim over, invading every department of the self. When the mind's loftiest and most ideal thought, its conscious vivid aspiration, has been united with the more robust qualities of the natural man; then, and only then, we have the material for the making of a possible saint.

We must also remember that, important as our primitive and instinctive life may be—and we should neither despise nor neglect it—its religious impulses, taken alone, no more represent the full range of man's spiritual possibilities than the life of the hunting tribe or the African kraal represent his full social possibilities. We may, and should, acknowledge and learn from our psychic origins. We must never be content to rest in them. Though in many respects, mental as well as physical, we are animals still; yet we are animals with a possible future in the making, both corporate and individual, which we cannot yet define. All other levels of life assure us that the impulsive nature is peculiarly susceptible to education. Not only can the whole group of instincts which help self-fulfilment be directed to higher levels, united and subdued to a dominant emotional interest; but merely instinctive actions can, by repetition and control, be raised to the level of habit and be given improved precision and complexity. This, of course, is a primary function of devotional exercises; training the first blind instinct for God to the complex responses of the life of prayer. Instinct is at best a rough and ready tool of life: practice is required if it is to produce its best results. Observe, for instance, the poor efforts of the young bird to escape capture; and compare this with the finished performance of the parent.[18] Therefore in estimating man's capacity for spiritual response, we must reckon not only his innate instinct for God, but also his capacity for developing this instinct on the level of habit; educating and using its latent powers to the best advantage. Especially on the contemplative side of life, education does great things for us; or would do, if we gave it the chance. Here, then, the rational mind and conscious will must play their part in that great business of human transcendence, which is man's function within the universal plan.

It is true that the deep-seated human tendency to God may best be understood as the highest form of that out-going instinctive craving of the psyche for more life and love which, on whatever level it be experienced, is always one. But some external stimulus seems to be needed, if this deep tendency is to be brought up into consciousness; and some education, if it is to be fully expressed. This stimulus and this education, in normal cases, are given by tradition; that is to say, by religious belief and practice. Or they may come from the countless minor and cumulative suggestions which life makes to us, and which few of us have the subtlety to analyze. If these suggestions of tradition or environment are met by resistance, either of the moral or intellectual order, whilst yet the deep instinct for full life remains unsatisfied, the result is an inner conflict of more or less severity; and as a rule, this is only resolved and harmony achieved through the crisis of conversion, breaking down resistances, liberating emotion and reconciling inner craving with outer stimulus. There is, however, nothing spiritual in the conversion process itself. It has its parallel in other drastic readjustments to other levels of life; and is merely a method by which selves of a certain type seem best able to achieve the union of feeling, thought, and will necessary to stability.

Now we have behind us and within us all humanity's funded instinct for the Divine, all the racial habits and traditions of response to the Divine. But its valid thought about the Divine comes as yet to very little. Thus we see that the author of "The Cloud of Unknowing" spoke as a true psychologist when he said that "a secret blind love pressing towards God" held more hope of success than mere thought can ever do; "for He may well be loved but not thought—by love He may be gotten and holden, but by thought never."[19] Nevertheless, if that consistency of deed and belief which is essential to full power is to be achieved by us, every man's conception of the God Whom he serves ought to be the very best of which he is capable. Because ideas which we recognize as partial or primitive have called forth the richness and devotion of other natures, we are not therefore excused from trying all things and seeking a Reality which fulfils to the utmost our craving for truth and beauty, as well, as our instinct for good. It is easy, natural, and always comfortable for the human mind to sink back into something just a little bit below its highest possible. On one hand to wallow in easy loves, rest in traditional formulæ, or enjoy a "moving type of devotion" which makes no intellectual demand. On the other, to accept without criticism the sceptical attitude of our neighbours, and keep safely in the furrow of intelligent agnosticism.

Religious people have a natural inclination to trot along on mediocre levels; reacting pleasantly to all the usual practices, playing down to the hopes and fears of the primitive mind, its childish craving for comfort and protection, its tendency to rest in symbols and spells, and satisfying its devotional inclinations by any "long psalter unmindfully mumbled in the teeth."[20] And a certain type of intelligent people have an equally natural tendency to dismiss, without further worry, the traditional notions of the past. In so far as all this represents a slipping back in the racial progress, it has the character of sin: at any rate, it lacks the true character of spiritual life. Such life involves growth, sublimation, the constant and difficult redirection of energy from lower to higher levels; a real effort to purge motive, see things more truly, face and resolve the conflict between the deep instinctive and the newer rational life. Hence, those who realize the nature of their own mental processes sin against the light if they do not do with them the very best that they possibly can: and the penalty of this sin must be a narrowing of vision, an arrest. The laws of apperception apply with at least as much force to our spiritual as to our sensual impressions: what we bring with us will condition what we obtain.

"We behold that which we are!" said Ruysbroeck long ago.[21] The mind's content and its ruling feeling-tone, says psychology, all its memories and desires, mingle with all incoming impressions, colour them and condition those which our consciousness selects. This intervention of memory and emotion in our perceptions is entirely involuntary; and explains why the devotee of any specific creed always finds in the pure immediacy of religious experience the special marks of his own belief. In most acts of perception—and probably, too, in the intuitional awareness of religious experience—that which the mind brings is bulkier if less important than that which it receives; and only the closest analysis will enable us to separate these two elements. Yet this machinery of apperception—humbling though its realization must be to the eager idealist—does not merely confuse the issue for us; or compel us to agnosticism as to the true content of religious intuition. On the contrary, its comprehension gives us the clue to many theological puzzles; whilst its existence enables us to lay hold of supersensual experiences we should otherwise miss, because it gives to us the means of interpreting them. Pure immediacy, as such, is almost ungraspable by us. As man, not as pure spirit, the High Priest entered the Holy of Holies: that is to say, he took to the encounter of the Infinite the finite machinery of sense. This limitation is ignored by us at our peril. The great mystics, who have sought to strip off all image and reach—as they say—the Bare Pure Truth, have merely become inarticulate in their effort to tell us what it was that they knew. "A light I cannot measure, goodness without form!" exclaims Jacopone da Todi.[22] "The Light of the *World*—the Good *Shepherd*," says St. John, bringing a richly furnished poetic consciousness to the vision of God; and at once gives us something on which to lay hold.

Generally speaking, it is only in so far as we bring with us a plan of the universe that we can make anything of it; and only in so far as we bring with us some idea of God, some feeling of desire for Him, can we apprehend Him—so true is it that we do, indeed, behold that which we are, find that which we seek, receive that for which we ask. Feeling, thought, and tradition must all contribute to the full working out of religious experience. The empty soul facing an unconditioned Reality may achieve freedom but assuredly achieves nothing else: for though the self-giving of Spirit is abundant, we control our own powers of reception. This lays on each self the duty of filling the mind with the noblest possible thoughts about God, refusing unworthy and narrow conceptions, and keeping alight the fire of His love. We shall find that which we seek: hence a richly stored religious consciousness, the lofty conceptions of the truth seeker, the vision of the artist, the boundless charity and joy in life of the lover of his kind, really contribute to the fulness of the spiritual life; both on its active and on its contemplative side. As the self reaches the first degrees of the prayerful or recollected state, memory-elements, released from the competition of realistic experience, enter the foreconscious field. Among these will be the stored remembrances of past meditations, reading, and experiences, all giving an affective tone conducive to new and deeper apprehensions. The pure in heart see God, because they bring with them that radiant and undemanding purity: because the storehouse of ancient memories, which each of us inevitably brings to that encounter, is free from conflicting desires and images, perfectly controlled by this feeling-tone.

It is now clear that all which we have so far considered supports, from the side of psychology, the demand of every religion for a drastic overhaul of the elements of character, a real repentance and moral purgation, as the beginning of all personal spiritual life. Man does not, as a rule, reach without much effort and suffering the higher levels of his psychic being. His old attachments are hard; complexes of which he is hardly aware must be broken up before he can use the forces which they enchain. He must, then, examine without flinching his impulsive life, and know what is in his heart, before he is in a position to change it. "The light which shows us our sins," says George Fox, "is the light that heals us." All those repressed cravings, those quietly unworthy motives, those mean acts which we instinctively thrust into the hiddenness and disguise or forget, must be brought to the surface and, in the language of psychology, "abreacted"; in the language of religion, confessed. The whole doctrine of repentance really hinges on this question of abreacting painful or wrongful experience instead of repressing it. The broken and contrite heart is the heart of which the hard complexes have been shattered by sorrow and love, and their elements brought up into consciousness and faced: and only the self which has endured this, can hope to be established in the free Spirit. It is a process of spiritual hygiene.

Psycho-analysis has taught us the danger of keeping skeletons in the cupboards of the soul, the importance of tracking down our real motives, of facing reality, of being candid and fearless in self-knowledge. But the emotional colour of this process when it is undertaken in the full conviction of the power and holiness of that life-force which we have not used as well as we might, and with a humble and loving consciousness of our deficiency, our falling short, will be totally different from the feeling state of those who conceive themselves to be searching for the merely animal sources of their mental and spiritual life. "Meekness in itself," says "The Cloud of Unknowing," "is naught else but a true knowing and feeling of a man's self as he is. For surely whoso might verily see and feel himself as he is, he should verily be meek. Therefore swink and sweat all that thou canst and mayst for to get thee a true knowing and feeling of thyself as thou art; and then I trow that soon after that thou shalt have a true knowing and feeling of God as he is."[23]

The essence, then, of repentance and purification of character consists first in the identification, and next in the sublimation of our instinctive powers and tendencies; their detachment from egoistic desires and dedication to new purposes. We should not starve or repress the abounding life within us; but, relieving it of its concentration on the here-and-now, give its attention and its passion a wider circle of interest over which to range, a greater love to which it can consecrate its growing powers. We do not yet know what the limit of such sublimation may be. But we do know that it is the true path of life's advancement, that already we owe to it our purest loves, our loveliest visions, and our noblest deeds. When such feeling, such vision and such act are united and transfigured in God, and find in contact with His living Spirit the veritable sources of their power; then, man will have resolved his inner conflict, developed his true potentialities, and live a harmonious because a spiritual life.

We end, therefore, upon this conception of the psyche as the living force within us; a storehouse of ancient memories and animal tendencies, yet plastic, adaptable, ever pressing on and ever craving for more life and more love. Only the life of reality, the life rooted in communion with God, will ever satisfy that hungry spirit, or provide an adequate objective for its persistent onward push.

---

1. Ennead IV. 8. 5.
2. De Imit. Christi, Bk. III, Cap. 53.
3. Boehme, "The Way to Christ," Pt. IV.
4. Unamuno has not hesitated to base the whole of religion on the instinct of self-preservation: but this must I think be regarded as an exaggerated view. See "The Tragic Sense of Life in Men and in Peoples," Caps. 3 and 4.
5. Boehme: "Six Theosophic Points," p. 98.
6. "The Cloud of Unknowing," Cap. 36.
7. E. Gardner: "St. Catherine of Siena," p. 20.
8. "Life of St. Teresa," by Herself, Cap. 30.
9. "Liberal and Mystical Writings of William Law" p. 59.
10. Jacopone da Todi, Lauda 90.
11. "Liberal and Mystical Writings of William Law," p. 123.
12. "Amor tu se'quel ama
    donde lo cor te ama."
    —Jacopone da Todi: Lauda 81.
13. Cf. Watts: "Echo Personalities," for several illustrations of this law.
14. Livingstone: "Mary Slessor of Calabar," p. 131.
15. "The Cloud of Unknowing," Cap, 40.

16. "And very often did He say unto me, 'Bride and daughter, sweet art thou unto Me, I love thee better than any other who is in the valley of Spoleto.'" ("The Divine Consolations of Blessed Angela of Foligno," p. 160.)
17. "The Spirit," edited by B.H. Streeter, p. 93.
18. Cf. B. Russell: "The Analysis of Mind," Cap. 2.
19. Op. cit., Cap. 6.
20. "Cloud of Unknowing," Cap. 37.
21. Ruysbroeck: "The Sparkling Stone," Cap. 9.
22. Lauda 91.
23. Op. cit., Cap. 13.

CHAPTER IV

PSYCHOLOGY AND THE LIFE OF THE SPIRIT (II) CONTEMPLATION AND SUGGESTION

In the last chapter we considered what the modern analysis of mind had to tell us about the nature of the spiritual life, the meaning of sin and of salvation. We now go on to another aspect of this subject: namely, the current conception of the unconscious mind as a dominant factor of our psychic life, and of the extent and the conditions in which its resources can be tapped, and its powers made amenable to the direction of the conscious mind. Two principal points must here be studied. The first is the mechanism of that which is called autistic thinking and its relation to religious experience: the second, the laws of suggestion and their bearing upon the spiritual life. Especially must we consider from this point of view the problems which are resumed under the headings of prayer, contemplation, and grace. We shall find ourselves compelled to examine the nature of meditation and recollection, as spiritual persons have always practised them; and, to give, if we can, a psychological account of many of their classic conceptions and activities. We shall therefore be much concerned with those experiences which are often called mystical, but which I prefer to call in general contemplative and intuitive; because they extend, as we shall find, without a break from the simplest type of mental prayer, the most general apprehensions of the Spirit, to the most fully developed examples of religious mono-ideism. To place all those intuitions and perceptions of which God or His Kingdom are the objects in a class apart from all other intuitions and perceptions, and call them "mystical," is

THE LIFE OF THE SPIRIT AND THE LIFE OF TO-DAY

really to beg the question from the start. The psychic mechanisms involved in them are seen in action in many other types of mental activity; and will not, in my opinion, be understood until they are removed from the category of the supernatural, and studied as the movements of the one spirit of life—here directed towards a transcendent objective. And further we must ever keep in mind, since we are now dealing with specific spiritual experiences, deeply exploring the contemplative soul, that though psychology can criticize these experiences, and help us to separate the wheat from the chaff—can tell us, too, a good deal about the machinery by which we lay hold of them, and the best way to use it—it cannot explain the experiences, pronounce upon their Object, or reduce that Object to its own terms.

We may some day have a valid psychology of religion, though we are far from it yet: but when we do, it will only be true within its own system of reference. It will deal with the fact of the spiritual life from one side only. And as a discussion of the senses and their experience explains nothing about the universe by which these senses are impressed, so all discussion of spiritual faculty and experience remains within the human radius and neither invalidates nor accounts for the spiritual world. When the psychologist has finished telling us all that he knows about the rules which govern our mental life, and how to run it best, he is still left face to face with the mystery of that life, and of that human power of surrender to Spiritual Reality which is the very essence of religion. Humility remains, therefore, not only the most becoming but also the most scientific attitude for investigators in this field. We must, then, remember the inevitably symbolic nature of the language which we are compelled to use in our attempt to describe these experiences; and resist all temptation to confuse the handy series of labels with which psychology has furnished us, with the psychic unity to which they will be attached.

Perhaps the most fruitful of all our recent discoveries in the mental region will turn out to be that which is gradually revealing to us the extent and character of the unconscious mind; and the possibility of tapping its resources, bending its plastic shape to our own mould. It seems as though the laws of its being are at last beginning to be understood; giving a new content to the ancient command "Know thyself." We are learning that psycho-therapy, which made such immense strides during the war, is merely one of the directions in which this knowledge may be used, and this control exercised by us. That regnancy of spirit over matter towards which all idealists must look, is by way of coming at least to a partial fulfilment in this control of the conscious over the unconscious, and thus over the bodily life. Such control is indeed an aspect of our human freedom, of the creative power which has been put into our hands. In all this religion must be interested: because, once more, it is the business of religion to regenerate the whole man and win him for Reality.

If we could get rid of the idea that the unconscious is a separate, and in some sort hostile or animal entity set over against the conscious mind; and realize that it is, simply, our whole personality, with the exception of the scrap that happens at any moment to be in consciousness—then, perhaps, we should more easily grasp the importance of exploring and mobilizing its powers. As it is, most of us behave like the owners of a well-furnished room, who ignore every aspect of it except the window looking out upon the street. This we keep polished, and drape with the best curtains that we can afford. But the room upon which we sedulously turn our backs contains all that we have inherited, all that we have accumulated, many tools which are rusting for want of use; machinery too which, left to itself, may function satisfactorily, or may get out of order and work to results that we neither desire nor dream. The room is twilit. Only by the window is a little patch of light. Beyond this there is a fringe of vague, fluctuating, sometimes prismatic radiance: an intermediate region, where the images and things which most interest us have their place, just within range, or the fringe of the field of consciousness. In the darkest corners the machinery that we do not understand, those possessions of which we are least proud, and those pictures we hate to look at, are hidden away.

This little parable represents, more or less, that which psychology means by the conscious, foreconscious, and unconscious regions of the psyche. It must not be pressed, or too literally interpreted; but it helps us to remember the graded character of our consciousness, its fluctuating level, and the fact that, as well as the outward-looking mind which alone we usually recognize, there is also the psychic matrix from which it has been developed, the inward-looking mind, caring for a variety of interests of which we hardly, as we say, think at all. We know as yet little about this mysterious psychic whole: the inner nature of which is only very incompletely given to us in the fluctuating experiences of consciousness. But we do know that it, too, receives at least a measure of the light and the messages coming in by the window of our wits: that it is the home of memory instinct and habit, the source of conduct, and that its control and modification form the major part of the training of character. Further, it is sensitive, plastic, accessible to impressions, and unforgetting.

THE LIFE OF THE SPIRIT AND THE LIFE OF TO-DAY

Consider now that half-lit region which is called the foreconscious mind; for this is of special interest to the spiritual life. It is, in psychological language, the region of autistic as contrasted with realistic thought.[1] That is to say, it is the agent of reverie and meditation; it is at work in all our brooding states, from day-dream to artistic creation. Such autistic thought is dominated not by logic or will, but by feeling. It achieves its results by intuition, and has its reasons which the surface mind knows not of. Here, in this fringe-region—which alone seems fully able to experience adoration and wonder, or apprehend the values we call holiness, beauty or love—is the source of that intuition of the heart to which the mystic owes the love which is knowledge, and the knowledge which is love. Here is the true home of inspiration and invention. Here, by a process which is seldom fully conscious save in its final stages, the poet's creations are prepared, and thence presented in the form of inspiration to the reason; which—if he be a great artist—criticizes them, before they are given as poems to the world. Indeed, in all man's apprehensions of the transcendental these two states of the psyche must co-operate if he is to realize his full powers: and it is significant that to this foreconscious region religion, in its own special language, has always invited him to retreat, if he would know his own soul and thus commune with his God. Over and over again it assures him under various metaphors, that he must turn within, withdraw from the window, meet the inner guest; and such a withdrawal is the condition of all contemplation.

Consider the opening of Jacob Boehme's great dialogue on the Supersensual Life.

"The Scholar said to his Master: How may I come to the supersensual life, that I may see God and hear Him speak?

"His Master said: When thou canst throw thyself for a moment into that where no creature dwelleth, then thou hearest what God speaketh.

"The Scholar said: Is that near at hand or far off?

"The Master said: It is in thee, if thou canst for a while cease from all thinking and willing, thou shalt hear the unspeakable words of God.

"The Scholar said: How can I hear when I stand still from thinking and willing?

"The Master said: When thou standest still from the thinking and willing of self, then the eternal hearing, seeing and speaking will be revealed in thee."[2]

In this passage we have a definite invitation to retreat from volitional to affective thought: from the window to the quiet place where "no creature dwelleth," and in Patmore's phrase "the night of thought becomes the light of perception."[3] This fringe-region or foreconscious is in fact the organ of contemplation, as the realistic outward looking mind is the organ of action. Most men go through life without conceiving, far less employing, the rich possibilities which are implicit in it. Yet here, among the many untapped resources of the self, lie our powers of response to our spiritual environment: powers which are kept by the tyrannical interests of everyday life below the threshold of full consciousness, and never given a chance to emerge. Here take place those searching experiences of the "inner life" which seem moonshine or morbidity to those who have not known them.

The many people who complain that they have no such personal religious experience, that the spiritual world is shut to them, are usually found to have expected this experience to be given to them without any deliberate and sustained effort on their own part. They have lived from childhood to maturity at the little window of consciousness and have never given themselves the opportunity of setting up correspondences with any other world than that of sense. Yet all normal men and women possess, at least in a rudimentary form, some intuition of the transcendental; shown in their power of experiencing beauty or love. In some it is dominant, emerging easily and without help; in others it is latent and must be developed in the right way. In others again it may exist in virtual conflict with a strongly realistic outlook; gathering way until it claims its rights at last in a psychic storm. Its emergence, however achieved, is a part—and for our true life, by far the most important part—of that outcropping and overflowing into consciousness of the marginal faculties which is now being recognized as essential to all artistic and creative activities; and as playing, too, a large part in the regulation of mental and bodily health.

All the great religions have implicitly understood—though without analysis—the vast importance of these spiritual intuitions and faculties lying below the surface of the everyday mind; and have perfected machinery tending to secure their release and their training. This is of two kinds: first, religious ceremonial, addressing itself to corporate feeling; next the discipline of meditation and prayer, which educates the individual to the same ends, gradually developing the powers of the foreconscious region, steadying them, and bringing them under the control of the purified will. Without some such education, widely as its details may vary, there can be no real living of the spiritual life.

> *"A going out into the life of sense*
> *Prevented the exercise of earnest realization."*[4]

Psychologists sometimes divide men into the two extreme classes of extroverts and introverts. The extrovert is the typical active; always leaning out of the window and setting up contacts with the outside world. His thinking is mainly realistic. That is to say, it deals with the data of sense. The introvert is the typical contemplative, predominantly interested in the inner world. His thinking is mainly autistic, dealing with the results of intuition and feeling, working these up into new structures and extorting from them new experiences. He is at home in the foreconscious, has its peculiar powers under control; and instinctively obedient to the mystic command to sink into the ground of the soul, he leans towards those deep wells of his own being which plunge into the unconscious foundations of life. By this avoidance of total concentration on the sense world—though material obtained from it must as a matter of fact enter into all, even his most "spiritual" creations—he seems able to attend to the messages which intuition picks up from other levels of being. It is significant that nearly all spiritual writers use this very term of introversion, which psychology has now adopted as the most accurate that it can find, in a favourable, indeed laudatory, sense. By it they intend to describe the healthy expansion of the inner life, the development of the soul's power of attention to the spiritual, which is characteristic of those real men and women of prayer whom Ruysbroeck describes as:—

> *"Gazing inward with an eye uplifted and open to the*
> *Eternal Truth*
> *Inwardly abiding in simplicity and stillness and in utter*
> *peace."*[5]

It is certain that no one who wholly lacks this power of retreat from the surface, and has failed thus to mobilize his foreconscious energies, can live a spiritual life. This is why silence and meditation play so large a part in all sane religious discipline. But the ideal state, a state answering to that rhythm of work and prayer which should be the norm of a mature spirituality, is one in which we have achieved that mental flexibility and control which puts us in full possession of our autistic *and* our realistic powers; balancing and unifying the inner and the outer world.

This being so, it is worth while to consider in more detail the character of foreconscious thought.

Foreconscious thinking, as it commonly occurs in us, with its unchecked illogical stream of images and ideas, moving towards no assigned end, combined in no ordered chain, is merely what we usually call day-dream. But where a definite wish or purpose, an *end*, dominates this reverie and links up its images and ideas into a cycle, we get in combination all the valuable properties both of affective and of directed thinking; although the reverie or contemplation place in the fringe-region of our mental life, and in apparent freedom from the control of the conscious reason. The object of recollection and meditation, which are the first stages of mental prayer, is to set going such a series and to direct it towards an assigned end: and this first inward-turning act and self-orientation are voluntary, though the activities which they set up are not. "You must know, my daughters," says St. Teresa, "that this is no supernatural act but depends on our will; and that therefore we can do it, with that ordinary assistance of God which we need for all our acts and even for our good thoughts."[6]

Consider for a moment what happens in prayer. I pass over the simple recitation of verbal prayers, which will better be dealt with when we come to consider the institutional framework of the spiritual life. We are now concerned with mental prayer or orison; the simplest of those degrees of contemplation which may pass gradually into mystical experience, and are at least in some form a necessity of any real and actualized spiritual life. Such prayer is well defined by the mystics, as "a devout intent directed to God."[7] What happens in it? All writers on the science of prayer observe, that the first necessity is Recollection; which, in a rough and ready way, we may render as concentration, or perhaps in the special language of psychology as "contention." The mind is called in from external interests and distractions, one by one the avenues of sense are closed, till the hunt of the world is hardly perceived by it. I need not labour this description, for it is a state of which we must all have experience: but those who wish to see it described with the precision of genius, need only turn to St. Teresa's "Way of Perfection." Having achieved this, we pass gradually into the condition of deep withdrawal variously called Simplicity or Quiet; a state in which the attention is quietly and without effort directed to God, and the whole self as it were held in His presence. This presence is given, dimly or clearly, in intuition. The actual prayer used will probably consist—again to use technical language—of "affective acts and aspirations"; short phrases repeated and held, perhaps expressing penitence, humility, adoration or love, and for the praying self charged with profound significance.

"If we would intentively pray for getting of good," says "The Cloud of Unknowing," "let us cry either with word or with thought or with desire, nought else nor on more words but this word God.... Study thou not for no words, for so shouldst thou never come to thy purpose nor to this work, for it is never got by study, but all only by grace."[8]

Now the question naturally arises, how does this recollected state, this alogical brooding on a spiritual theme, exceed in religions value the orderly saying of one's prayers? And the answer psychology suggests is, that more of us, not less, is engaged in such a spiritual act: that not only the conscious attention, but the foreconscious region too is then thrown open to the highest sources of life. We are at last learning to recognize the existence of delicate mental processes which entirely escape the crude methods of speech. Reverie as a genuine thought process is beginning to be studied with the attention it deserves, and new understanding of prayer must result. By its means powers of perception and response ordinarily latent are roused to action; and thus the whole life is enriched. That faculty in us which corresponds, not with the busy life of succession but with the eternal sources of power, gets its chance. "Though the soul," says Von Hügel, "cannot abidingly abstract itself from its fellows, it can and ought frequently to recollect itself in a simple sense of God's presence. Such moments of direct preoccupation with God alone bring a deep refreshment and simplification to the soul."[9]

True silence, says William Penn, of this quiet surrender to reality, "is rest to the mind, and is to the spirit what sleep is to the body; nourishment and refreshment."[10] Psychology endorses the constant statements of all religions of the Spirit, that no one need hope to live a spiritual life who cannot find a little time each day for this retreat from the window, this quiet and loving waiting upon the unseen "with the forces of the soul," as Ruysbroeck puts it, "gathered into unity of the Spirit."[11] Under these conditions, and these only, the intuitive, creative, artistic powers are captured and dedicated to the highest ends: and in these powers rather than the rational our best chance of apprehending eternal values abides, "Taste and *see* that the Lord is sweet." "Be still! be still! and *know* that I am God!"

Since, then, the foreconscious mind and its activities are of such paramount interest to the spiritual life, we may before we go on glance at one or two of its characteristics. And first we notice that the fact that the foreconscious is, so to speak, in charge in the mental and contemplative type of prayer explains why it is that even the most devout persons are so constantly tormented by distractions whilst engaged in it. Very often, they are utterly unable to keep their attention fixed; and the reason of this is, that conscious attention and thought are not the faculties primarily involved. What is involved, is reverie coloured by feeling; and this tends to depart from its assigned end and drift into mere day-dream, if the emotional tension slackens or some intruding image starts a new train of associations. The religious mind is distressed by this constant failure to look steadily at that which alone it wants to see; but the failure abides in the fact that the machinery used is affective, and obedient to the rise and fall of feeling rather than the control of the will. "By love shall He be gotten and holden, by thought never."

Next, consider for a moment the way in which the foreconscious does and must present its apprehensions to consciousness. Its cognitions of the spiritual are in the nature of pure immediacy, of uncriticized contacts: and the best and greatest of them seem to elude altogether that machinery of speech and image which has been developed through the life of sense. The well-known language of spiritual writers about the divine darkness or ignorance is an acknowledgment of this. God is "known darkly." Our experience of Eternity is "that of which nothing can be said." It is "beyond feeling" and "beyond knowledge," a certitude known in the ground of the soul, and so forth. It is indeed true that the spiritual world is for the human mind a transcendent world, does differ utterly in kind from the best that the world of succession is able to give us; as we know once for all when we establish a contact with it, however fleeting. But constantly the foreconscious—which, as we shall do well to remember, is the artistic region of the mind, the home of the poem, and the creative phantasy—works up its transcendent intuitions in symbolic form. For this purpose it sometimes uses the machinery of speech, sometimes that of image. As our ordinary reveries constantly proceed by way of an interior conversation or narrative, so the content of spiritual contemplation is often expressed in dialogue, in which memory and belief are fused with the fruit of perception. The "Dialogue of St. Catherine of Siena," the "Life of Suso," and the "Imitation of Christ," all provide beautiful examples of this; but indeed illustrations of it might be found in every school and period of religious literature.

Such inward dialogue, one of the commonest spontaneous forms of autistic thought, is perpetually resorted to by devout minds to actualize their consciousness of direct communion with God. I need not point out how easily and naturally it expresses for them that sense of a Friend and Companion, an indwelling power and support, which is perhaps their characteristic experience. "Blessed is that soul," says à Kempis, "that heareth the Lord speaking in him and taketh from His mouth the word of consolation. Blessed be those ears that receive of God's whisper and take no heed of the whisper of this world."[12] Though St. John of the Cross has reminded us with blunt candour that such persons are for the most part only talking to themselves, we need not deny the value of such a talking as a means of expressing the deeply known and intimate presence of Spirit. Moreover, the thoughts and words in which the contemplative expresses his sense of love and dedication reverberate as it were in the depths of the instinctive mind, now in this quietude thrown open to these influences: and the instinctive mind, as we have already seen, is the home of character and of habit formation.

Where there is a tendency to think in images rather than in words, the experiences of the Spirit may be actualized in the form of vision rather than of dialogue: and here again, memory and feeling will provide the material. Here we stand at the sources of religious art: which, when it is genuine, is a symbolic picture of the experiences of faith, and in those minds attuned to it may evoke again the memory or very presence of those experiences. But many minds are, as it were, their own religious artists; and build up for themselves psychic structures answering to their intuitive apprehensions. So vivid may these structures sometimes be for them that —to revert again to our original simile—the self turns from the window and the realistic world without, and becomes for the time wholly concentrated on the symbolic drama or picture within the room; which abolishes all awareness of the everyday world. When this happens in a small way, we have what might be called a religious day-dream of more or less beauty and intensity; such as most devout people who tend to visualization have probably known. When the break with the external world is complete, we get those ecstatic visions in which mystics of a certain type actualize their spiritual intuitions. The Bible is full of examples of this. Good historic instances are the visions of Mechthild of Magdeburg or Angela of Foligno. The first contain all the elements of drama, the last cover a wide symbolic and emotional field. Those who have read Canon Streeter's account of the visions of the Sadhu Sundar Singh will recognize them as being of this type.[13]

I do not wish to go further than this into the abnormal and extreme types of religious autism; trance, ecstasy and so forth. Our concern is with the norm of the spiritual life, as it exists to-day and as all may live it. But it is necessary to realize that image and vision do within limits represent a perfectly genuine way of doing things, which is inevitable for deeply spiritual selves of a certain type; and that it is neither good psychology nor good Christianity, lightly to dismiss as superstition or hysteria the pictured world of symbol in which our neighbour may live and save his soul. The symbolic world of traditional piety, with its angels and demons, its friendly saints, its spatial heaven, may conserve and communicate spiritual values far better than the more sophisticated universe of religious philosophy. We may be sure that both are more characteristic of the image-making and structure-building tendencies of the mind, than they are of the ultimate and for us unknowable reality of things. Their value—or the value of any work of art which the foreconscious has contrived—abides wholly in the content: the quality of the material thus worked up. The rich nature, the purified love, capable of the highest correspondences, will express even in the most primitive duologue or vision the results of a veritable touching and tasting of Eternal Life. Its psychic structures—however logic may seek to discredit them—will convey spiritual fact, have the quality which the mystics mean when they speak of illumination. The emotional pietist will merely ramble among the religious symbols and phrases with which the devout memory is stored. It is true that the voice or the picture, surging up as it does into the field of consciousness, seems to both classes to have the character of a revelation. The pictures unroll themselves automatically and with amazing authority and clearness, the conversation is with Another than ourselves; or in more generalized experiences, such as the sense of the Divine Presence, the contact is with another order of life. But the crucial question which religion asks must be, does fresh life flow in from those visions and contacts, that intercourse? Is transcendental feeling involved in them? "What fruits dost thou bring back from this thy vision?" says Jacopone da Todi;[14] and this remains the only real test by which to separate day-dreams from the vitalizing act of contemplation. In the first we are abandoned to a delightful, and perhaps as it seems holy or edifying vagrancy of thought. In the second, by a deliberate choice and act of will, foreconscious thinking is set going and directed towards an assigned end: the apprehending and actualizing of our deepest intuition of God. In it, a great region of the mind usually ignored by us and left to chance, yet source of many choices and deeds, and capable of much purifying pain, is put to its true work: and it is work which must be humbly, regularly and faithfully performed. It is to this region that poetry, art and music—and even, if I dare say so, philosophy—make their fundamental appeal. No life is whole and harmonized in which it has not taken its right place.

We must now go on—and indeed, any psychological study of prayerful experience must lead us on—to the subject of suggestion, and its relation to the inner life. By suggestion of course is here meant, in conformity with current psychological doctrine, the process by which an idea enters the deeper and unconscious psychic levels and there becomes fruitful. Its real nature, and in consequence something of its far-reaching importance, is now beginning to be understood by us: a fact of great moment for both the study and the practice of the spiritual life. Since the transforming work of the Spirit must be done through man's ordinary psychic machinery and in conformity with the laws which govern it, every such increase in our knowledge of that machinery must serve the interests of religion, and show its teachers the way to success. Suggestion is usually said to be of two kinds. The first is hetero-suggestion, in which the self-realizing idea is received either wittingly or unwittingly from the outer world. During the whole of our conscious lives for good or evil we are at the mercy of such hetero-suggestions, which are being made to us at every moment by our environment; and they form, as we shall afterwards see, a dominant factor in corporate religious exercises. The second type is auto-suggestion. In this, by means of the conscious mind, an idea is implanted in the unconscious and there left to mature. Thus do willingly accepted beliefs, religious, social, or scientific, gradually and silently permeate the whole being and show their results in character.

A little reflection shows, however, that these two forms of suggestion shade into one another; and that no hetero-suggestion, however impressively given, becomes active in us until we have in some sort accepted it and transformed it into an auto-suggestion. Theology expresses this fact in its own special language, when it says that the will must co-operate with grace if it is to be efficacious. Thus the primacy of the will is safeguarded. It stands, or should stand, at the door; selecting from among the countless dynamic suggestions, good and bad, which life pours in on us, those which serve the best interests of the self.

As a rule, men take little trouble to sort out the incoming suggestions. They allow uncriticized beliefs and prejudices, the ideas of hatred, anxiety or ill-health, free entrance. They fail to seize and affirm the ideas of power, renovation, joy. They would be more careful, did they grasp more fully the immense and often enduring effect of these accepted suggestions; the extent in which the fundamental, unreasoning psychic deeps are plastic to ideas. Yet this plasticity is exhibited in daily life first under the emotional form of sympathy, response to the suggestion of other peoples' feeling-states; and next under the conative form of imitation, active acceptance of the suggestion made by their appearance, habits, deeds. All political creeds, panics, fashion and good form witness to the overwhelming power of suggestion. We are so accustomed to this psychic contagion that we fail to realize the strangeness of the process: but it is now known to reach a degree previously unsuspected, and of which we have not yet found the limits.

In the religious sphere, the more sensational demonstrations of this psychic suggestibility have long been notorious. Obvious instances are those ecstatics—some of them true saints, some only religious invalids—whose continuous and ardent meditation on the Cross produced in them the actual bodily marks of the Passion of Christ. In less extreme types, perpetual dwelling on this subject, together with that eager emotional desire to be united with the sufferings of the Redeemer which mediæval religion encouraged, frequently modified the whole life of the contemplative; shaping the plastic mind, and often the body too, to its own mould. A good historic example of this law of religious suggestibility is the case of Julian of Norwich. As a young girl, Julian prayed that she might have an illness at thirty years of age, and also a closer knowledge of Christ's pains. She forgot the prayer: but it worked below the threshold as forgotten suggestions often do, and when she was thirty the illness came. Its psychic origin can still be recognized in her own candid account of it; and with the illness the other half of that dynamic prayer received fulfilment, in those well-known visions of the Passion to which we owe the "Revelations of Divine Love."[15]

This is simply a striking instance of a process which is always taking place in every one of us, for good or evil. The deeper mind opens to all who knock; provided only that the new-comers be not the enemies of some stronger habit or impression already within. To suggestions which coincide with the self's desires or established beliefs it gives an easy welcome; and these, once within, always tend to self-realization. Thus the French Carmelite Thérèse de l'Enfant-Jésus, once convinced that she was destined to be a "victim of love," began that career of suffering which ended in her death at the age of twenty-four.[16] The lives of the Saints are full of incidents explicable on the same lines: exhibiting again and again the dramatic realization of traditional ideas or passionate desires. We see therefore that St. Paul's admonition "Whatsoever things are pure, whatsoever things are lovely, whatsoever things be of good report, think on these things" is a piece of practical advice of which the importance can hardly be exaggerated; for it deals with the conditions under which man makes his own mentality.

Suggestion, in fact, is one of the most powerful agents either of self-destruction or of self-advancement which are within our grasp: and those who speak of the results of psycho-therapy, or the certitudes of religious experience, as "mere suggestion" are unfortunate in their choice of an adjective. If then we wish to explore all those mental resources which can be turned to the purposes of the spiritual life, this is one which we must not neglect. The religious idea, rightly received into the mind and reinforced by the suggestion of regular devotional exercises, always tends to realize itself. "Receive His leaven," says William Penn, "and it will change thee, His medicine and it will cure thee. He is as infallible as free; without money and with certainty. Yield up the body, soul and spirit to Him that maketh all things new: new heaven and new earth, new love, new joy, new peace, new works, a new life and conversation."[17] This is fine literature, but it is more important to us to realize that it is also good psychology: and that here we are given the key to those amazing regenerations of character which are the romance and glory of the religious life. Pascal's too celebrated saying, that if you will take holy water regularly you will presently believe, witnesses on another level to the same truth.

Fears have been expressed that, by such an application of the laws of suggestion to religious experience, we shall reduce religion itself to a mere favourable subjectivism, and identify faith with suggestibility. But here the bearing of this series of facts on bodily health provides us with a useful analogy. Bodily health is no illusion. It does not consist in merely thinking that we are well, but is a real condition of well-being and of power; depending on the state of our tissues and correct balance and working of our physical and psychical life. And this correct and wholesome working will be furthered and steadied—or if broken may often be restored—by good suggestions; it may be disturbed by bad suggestions; because the controlling factor of life is mind, not chemistry, and mind is plastic to ideas. So too the life of the Spirit is a concrete fact; a real response to a real universe. But this concrete life of faith, with its growth and its experiences, its richly various working of one principle in every aspect of existence, its correspondences with the Eternal World, its definitely ontological references, is lived here and now; in and through the self's psychic life, and indeed his bodily life too—a truth which is embodied in sacramentalism. Therefore, sharing as it does life's plastic character, it too is amenable to suggestion and can be helped or hindered by it. It is indeed characteristic of those in whom this life is dominant, that they are capable of receiving and responding to the highest and most vivifying suggestions which the universe in its totality pours in on us. This movement of response, often quietly overlooked, is that which makes them not spiritual hedonists but men and women of prayer. Grace—to give these suggestions of Spirit their conventional name—is perpetually beating in on us. But if it is to be inwardly realized, the Divine suggestion must be transformed by man's will and love into an auto-suggestion; and this is what seems to happen in meditation and prayer.

Everything indeed points to a very close connection between what might be called the mechanism of prayer and of suggestion. To say this, is in no way to minimize the transcendental character of prayer. In both states there is a spontaneous or deliberate throwing open of the deeper mind to influences which, fully accepted, tend to realize themselves. Look at the directions given by all great teachers of prayer and contemplation; and these two acts, rightly performed, fuse one with the other, they are two aspects of the single act of communion with God. Look at their insistence on a stilling and recollecting of the mind, on surrender, a held passivity not merely limp but purposeful: on the need of meek yielding to a greater inflowing power, and its regenerating suggestions. Then compare this with the method by which health-giving suggestions are made to the bodily life. "In the deeps of the soul His word is spoken." Is not this an exact description of the inward work of the self-realizing idea of holiness, received in the prayer of quiet into the unconscious mind, and there experienced as a transforming power? I think that we may go even further than this, and say that grace, is, in effect, the direct suggestion of the spiritual affecting our soul's life. As we are commonly docile to the countless hetero-suggestions, some of them helpful, some weakening, some actually perverting, which our environment is always making to us; so we can and should be so spiritually suggestible that we can receive those given to us by all-penetrating Divine life. What is generally called sin, especially in the forms of self-sufficiency, lack of charity and the indulgence of the senses, renders us recalcitrant to these living suggestions of the Spirit. The opposing qualities, humility, love and purity, make us as we say accessible to grace.

THE LIFE OF THE SPIRIT AND THE LIFE OF TO-DAY

"Son," says the inward voice to Thomas à Kempis, "My grace is precious, and suffereth not itself to be mingled with strange things nor earthly consolations. Wherefore it behoveth thee to cast away impediments to grace, if thou willest to receive the inpouring thereof. Ask for thyself a secret place, love to dwell alone with thyself, seek confabulation of none other ... put the readiness for God before all other things, for thou canst not both take heed to Me and delight in things transitory.... This grace is a light supernatural and a special gift of God, and a proper sign of the chosen children of God, and the earnest of everlasting health; for God lifteth up man from earthly things to love heavenly things, and of him that is fleshly maketh a spiritual man."[18] Could we have a more vivid picture than this of the conditions of withdrawal and attention under which the psyche is most amenable to suggestion, or of the inward transfiguration worked by a great self-realizing idea? Such transfiguration has literally on the physical plane caused the blind to see, the deaf to hear, the dumb to speak: and it seems to me that it is to be observed operating on highest levels in the work of salvation. When further à Kempis prays "Increase in me more grace, that I may fulfil Thy word and make perfect mine own health" is he not describing the right balance to be sought between our surrender to the vivifying suggestions of grace and our appropriation and manly use of them? This is no limp acquiescence and merely infantile dependence, but another aspect of the vital balance between the indrawing and outgiving of power; and one of the main functions of prayer is to promote in us that spiritually suggestible state in which, as Dionysius the Areopagite says, we are "receptive of God."

It is, then, worth our while from the point of view of the spiritual life to inquire into the conditions in which a suggestion is most likely to be received and realized by us. These conditions, as psychologists have so far defined them, can be resumed under the three heads of quiescence, attention and feeling: outstanding characteristics, as I need not point out, of the state of prayer, all of which can be illustrated from the teaching and experience of the mystics.

First, let us take *Quiescence*. In order fully to lay open the unconscious to the influence of suggested ideas, the surface mind must be called in from its responses to the outer world, or in religious language recollected, till the hum of that world is hardly perceived by it. The body must be relaxed, making no demands on the machinery controlling the motor system; and the conditions in general must be those of complete mental and bodily rest. Here is the psychological equivalent of that which spiritual writers call the Quiet: a state defined by one of them as "a rest most busy." "Those who are in this prayer," says St. Teresa, "wish their bodies to remain motionless, for it seems to them that at the least movement they will lose their sweet peace."[19] Others say that in this state we "stop the wheel of imagination," leave all that we can think, sink into our nothingness or our ground. In Ruysbroeck's phrase, we are "inwardly abiding in simplicity and stillness and utter peace";[20] and this is man's state of maximum receptivity. "The best and noblest way in which thou mayst come into this work and life," says Meister Eckhart, "is by keeping silence and letting God work and speak ... when we simply keep ourselves receptive we are more perfect than when at work."[21]

But this preparatory state of surrendered quiet must at once be qualified by the second point: *Attention*. It is based upon the right use of the will, and is not a limp yielding to anything or nothing. It has an ordained deliberate aim, is a behaviour-cycle directed to an end; and this it is that marks out the real and fruitful quiet of the contemplative from the non-directed surrender of mere quietism. "Nothing," says St. Teresa, "is learnt without a little pains. For the love of God, sisters, account that care well employed that ye shall bestow on this thing."[22]

The quieted mind must receive and hold, yet without discursive thought, the idea which it desires to realize; and this idea must interest and be real for it, so that attention is concentrated on it spontaneously. The more completely the idea absorbs us, the greater its transforming power: when interest wavers, the suggestion begins to lose ground. In spite of her subsequent relapse into quietism Madame Guyon accurately described true quiet when she said, "Our activity should consist in endeavouring to acquire and maintain such a state as may be most susceptible of divine impressions, most flexible to all the operations of the Eternal Word."[23] Such concentration can be improved by practice; hence the value of regular meditation and contemplation to those who are in earnest about the spiritual life, the quiet and steady holding in the mind of the thought which it is desired to realize.

Psycho-therapists tell us that, having achieved quiescence, we should rapidly and rythmically, but with intention, repeat the suggestion that we wish to realize; and that the shorter, simpler and more general this verbal formula, the more effective it will be.[24] The spiritual aspect of this law was well understood by the mediæval mystics. Thus the author of "The Cloud of Unknowing" says to his disciple, "Fill thy spirit with ghostly meaning of this word Sin, and without any special beholding unto any kind of sin, whether it be venial or deadly. And cry thus ghostly ever upon one: Sin! Sin! Sin! out! out! out! This ghostly cry is better learned of God by the proof than of any man by word. For it is best when it is in pure spirit, without special thought or any pronouncing of word. On the same manner shalt thou do with this little word God: and mean God all, and all God, so that nought work in thy wit and in thy will but only God."[25] Here the directions are exact, and such as any psychologist of the present day might give. So too, religious teachers informed by experience have always ascribed a special efficacy to "short acts" of prayer and aspiration: phrases repeated or held in the mind, which sum up and express the self's penitence, love, faith or adoration, and are really brief, articulate suggestions parallel in type to those which Baudouin recommends to us as conducive to bodily well-being.[26] The repeated affirmation of Julian of Norwich "All shall be well! all shall be well! all shall be well!"[27] fills all her revelations with its suggestion of joyous faith; and countless generations of Christians have thus applied to their soul's health those very methods by which we are now enthusiastically curing indigestion and cold in the head. The articulate repetition of such phrases increases their suggestive power; for the unconscious is most easily reached by way of the ear. This fact throws light on the immemorial insistence of all great religions on the peculiar value of vocal prayer, whether this be the *mantra* of the Hindu or the *dikr* of the Moslem; and explains the instinct which causes the Catholic Church to require from her priests the verbal repetition, not merely the silent reading of their daily office. Hence, too, there is real educative value, in such devotions as the rosary; and the Protestant Churches showed little psychological insight when they abandoned it. Such "vain" repetitions, however much the rational mind may dislike, discredit or denounce them, have power to penetrate and modify the deeper psychic levels; always provided that they conflict with no accepted belief, are weighted with meaning and desire, with the intent stretched towards God, and are not allowed to become merely mechanical—the standing danger alike of all verbal suggestion and all vocal prayer.

Here we touch the third character of effective suggestion: *Feeling*. When the idea is charged with emotion, it is far more likely to be realized. War neuroses have taught us the dreadful potency of the emotional stimulus of fear; but this power of feeling over the unconscious has its good side too. Here we find psychology justifying the often criticized emotional element of religion. Its function is to increase the energy of the idea. The cool, judicious type of belief will never possess the life-changing power of a more fervid, though perhaps less rational faith. Thus the state of corporate suggestibility generated in a revival and on which the success of that revival depends, is closely related to the emotional character of the appeal which is made. And, on higher levels, we see that the transfigured lives and heroic energies of the great figures of Christian history all represent the realization of an idea of which the heart was an impassioned love of God, subduing to its purposes all the impulses and powers of the inner man, "If you would truly know how these things come to pass," said St. Bonaventura, "ask it of desire not of intellect; of the ardours of prayer, not of the teaching of the schools."[28] More and more psychology tends to endorse the truth of these words.

Quiescence, attention, and emotional interest are then the conditions of successful suggestion. We have further to notice two characteristics which have been described by the Nancy school of psychologists; and which are of some importance for those who wish to understand the mechanism of religious experience. These have been called the law of Unconscious Teleology, and the law of Reversed Effort.

The law of unconscious teleology means that when an end has been effectively suggested to it, the unconscious mind will always tend to work towards its realization. Thus in psycho-therapeutics it is found that a general suggestion of good health made to the sick person is often enough. The doctor may not himself know enough about the malady to suggest stage by stage the process of cure. But he suggests that cure; and the necessary changes and adjustments required for its realization are made unconsciously, under the influence of the dynamic idea. Here the direction of "The Cloud of Unknowing," "Look that nothing live in thy working mind but a naked intent directed to God"[29]—suggesting as it does to the psyche the ontological Object of faith—strikingly anticipates the last conclusions of science. Further, a fervent belief in the end proposed, a conviction of success, is by no means essential. Far more important is a humble willingness to try the method, give it a chance. That which reason may not grasp, the deeper mind may seize upon and realize; always provided that the intellect does not set up resistances. This is found to be true in medical practice, and religious teachers have always declared it to be true in the spiritual sphere; holding obedience, humility, and a measure of resignation, not spiritual vision, to be the true requisites for the reception of grace, the healing and renovation of the soul. Thus acquiescence in belief, and loyal and steady co-operation in the corporate religious life are often seen to work for good in those who submit to them; though these may lack, as they frequently say, the "spiritual sense." And this happens, not by magic, but in conformity with psychological law.

This tendency of the unconscious self to realize without criticism a suggested end lays on religious teachers the obligation of forming a clear and vital conception of the spiritual ideals which they wish to suggest, whether to themselves in their meditations or to others by their teaching: to be sure that they are wholesome, and really tend to fullness of life. It should also compel each of us to scrutinize those religious thoughts and images which we receive and on which we allow our minds to dwell: excluding those that are merely sentimental, weak or otherwise unworthy, and holding fast the noblest and most beautiful that we can find. For these ideas, however generalized, will set up profound changes in the mind that receives them. Thus the wrong conception of self-immolation will be faithfully worked out by the unconscious—and has been too often in the past—in terms of misery, weakness, or disease. We remember how the idea of herself as a victim of love worked physical destruction in Thérèse de L'Enfant Jésus: and we shall never perhaps know all the havoc wrought by the once fashionable doctrines of predestination and of the total depravity of human nature. All this shows how necessary it is to put hopeful, manly, constructive conceptions before those whom we try to help or instruct; constantly suggesting to them not the weak and sinful things that they are, but the living and radiant things which they can become.

Further, this tendency of the received suggestion to work out its whole content for good or evil within the unconscious mind, shows the importance which we ought to attach to the tone of a religions service, and how close too many of our popular hymns are to what one might call psychological sin; stressing as they do a childish weakness love of shelter and petting, a neurotic shrinking from full human life, a morbid preoccupation with failure and guilt. Such hymns make devitalizing suggestions, adverse to the health and energy of the spiritual life; and are all the more powerful because they are sung collectively and in rhythm, and are cast in an emotional mould.[30] There was some truth in the accusation of the Indian teacher Ramakrishna, that the books of the Christians insisted too exclusively on sin. He said, "He who repeats again and again 'I am bound! I am bound!' remains in bondage. He who repeats day and night 'I am a sinner! I am a sinner!' becomes a sinner indeed."[31]

I go on to the law of Reversed Effort; a psychological discovery which seems to be of extreme importance for the spiritual life. Briefly this means, that when any suggestion has entered the unconscious mind and there become active, all our conscious and anxious resistances to it are not merely useless but actually tend to intensify it. If it is to be dislodged, this will not be accomplished by mere struggle but by the persuasive power of another and superior auto-suggestion. Further, in respect of any habit that we seek to establish, the more desperate our struggle and sense of effort, the smaller will be our success. In small matters we have all experienced the working of this law: in frustrated struggles to attend to that which does not interest us, to check a tiresome cough, to keep our balance when learning to ride a bicycle. But it has also more important applications. Thus it indicates that a deliberate struggle to believe, to overcome some moral weakness, to keep attention fixed in prayer, will tend to frustration: for this anxious effort gives body to our imaginative difficulties and sense of helplessness, fixing attention on the conflict, not on the desired end. True, if this end is to be achieved the will must be directed to it, but only in the sense of giving steadfast direction to the desires and acts of the self, keeping attention orientated towards the goal. The pull of imaginative desire, not the push of desperate effort, serves us best. St. Teresa well appreciated this law and applied it to her doctrine of prayer. "If your thought," she says to her daughters, "runs after all the fooleries of the world, laugh at it and leave it for a fool and continue in your quiet ... if you seek by force of arms to bring it to you, you lose the strength which you have against it."[32]

This same principle is implicitly recognized by those theologians who declare that man can "do nothing of himself," that mere voluntary struggle is useless, and regeneration comes by surrender to grace: by yielding, that is, to the inner urge, to those sources of power which flow in, but are not dragged in. Indications of its truth meet us everywhere in spiritual literature. Thus Jacob Boehme says, "Because thou strivest against that out of which thou art come, thou breakest thyself off with thy own willing from God's willing."[33] So too the constant invitations to let God work and speak, to surrender, are all invitations to cease anxious strife and effort and give the Divine suggestions their chance. The law of reversed effort, in fact, is valid on every level of life; and warns us against the error of making religion too grim and strenuous an affair. Certainly in all life of the Spirit the will is active, and must retain its conscious and steadfast orientation to God. Heroic activity and moral effort must form an integral part of full human experience. Yet it is clearly possible to make too much of the process of wrestling evil. An attention chiefly and anxiously concentrated on the struggle with sins and weaknesses, instead of on the eternal sources of happiness and power, will offer the unconscious harmful suggestions of impotence and hence tend to frustration. The early ascetics, who made elaborate preparations for dealing with temptations, got as an inevitable result plenty of temptations with which to deal. A sounder method is taught by the mystics. "When thoughts of sin press on thee," says "The Cloud of Unknowing," "look over their shoulders seeking another thing, the which thing is God."[34]

These laws of suggestion, taken together, all seem to point, one way. They exhibit the human self as living, plastic, changeful; perpetually modified by the suggestions pouring in on it, the experiences and intuitions to which it reacts. Every thought, prayer, enthusiasm, fear, is of importance to it. Nothing leaves it as it was before. The soul, said Boehme, stands both in heaven and in hell. Keep it perpetually busy at the window of the senses, feed it with unlovely and materialistic ideas, and those ideas will realize themselves. Give the contemplative faculty its chance, let it breathe at least for a few moments of each day the spiritual atmosphere of faith, hope and love, and the spiritual life will at least in some measure be realized by it.

---

1. On all this, cf. J. Varendonck, "The Psychology of Day-dreams."
2. Jacob Boehme: "The Way to Christ," Pt. IV.
3. Patmore: "The Rod, the Root and the Flower: Aurea Dicta," 13.
4. Ruysbroeck: "The Book of the XII Béguines," Cap. 6.
5. "The Book of the XII Béguines," Cap. 7.
6. "The Way of Perfection," Cap. 29.
7. "The Cloud of Unknowing," Cap. 39.
8. *Ibid.*
9. "Eternal Life," p. 396.
10. Penn: "No Cross, No Crown."
11. "The Book of the XII Béguines," Cap, 7.
12. De Imit. Christi, Bk. III, Cap. I
13. Streeter and Appasamy: "The Sadhu, a Study in Mysticism and Practical Religion," Pt. V.
14. Que frutti reducene de esta tua visione?
    Vita ordinata en onne nazione.
    —Jacopone da Todi: Lauda 79.
15. Julian of Norwich: "Revelations of Divine Love," Caps. 2, 3, 4.
16. "Soeur Thérèse de l'Enfant-Jésus," Cap. 8.
17. William Penn: "No Cross, No Crown."
18. De Imit. Christi, Bk. III, Cap. 58.
19. "Way of Perfection," Cap. 33.
20. "The Book of the XII Béguines," Cap. 7.
21. Meister Eckhart, Pred. I.
22. "The Way of Perfection," Cap. 29.
23. "A Short and Easy Method of Prayer," Cap. 21.

24. Baudouin: "Suggestion and Auto-Suggestion," Pt. II, Cap 6.
25. Op. cit. Cap. 40.
26. Baudouin: "Suggestion and Auto-Suggestion," loc. cit.
27. "Revelations of Divine Love," Cap. 27.
28. "De Itinerario Mentis in Deo," Cap. 7.
29. Op. cit., Cap. 43.
30. Hymns of the Weary Willie type: e.g.
    "O Paradise, O Paradise
    Who does not sigh for rest?"
    should never be sung in congregations where the average age is less than sixty. Equally unsuited to general use are those expressing disillusionment, anxiety, or impotence. Any popular hymnal will provide an abundance of examples.
31. Quoted by Pratt: "The Religious Consciousness," Cap. 7.
32. "The Way of Perfection," Cap. 31.
33. "The Way to Christ," Pt. IV.
34. Op. cit., Cap. 32.

CHAPTER V

INSTITUTIONAL RELIGION AND THE LIFE OF THE SPIRIT

So far, in considering what psychology had to tell us about the conditions in which our spiritual life can develop, and the mental machinery it can use, we have been, deliberately, looking at men one by one. We have left on one side all those questions which relate to the corporate aspect of the spiritual life, and its expression in religious institutions; that is to say, in churches and cults. We have looked upon it as a personal growth and response; a personal reception of, and self-orientation to, Reality. But we cannot get away from the fact that this regenerate life does most frequently appear in history associated with, or creating for itself, a special kind of institution. Although it is impossible to look upon it as the appearance of a favourable variation within the species, it is also just as possible to look upon it as the formation of a new herd or tribe. Where the variation appears, and in its sense of newness, youth and vigour breaks away from the institution within which it has arisen, it generally becomes the nucleus about which a new group is formed. So that individualism and gregariousness are both represented in the full life of the Spirit; and however personal its achievement may seem to us, it has also a definitely corporate and institutional aspect.

I now propose to take up this side of the subject, and try to suggest one or two lines of thought which may help us to discover the meaning and worth of such societies and institutions. For after all, some explanation is needed of these often strange symbolic systems, and often rigid mechanizations, imposed on the free responses to Eternal Reality which we found to constitute the essence of religious experience. Any one who has known even such direct communion with the Spirit as is possible to normal human nature must, if he thinks out the implications of his own experience, feel it to be inconsistent that this most universal of all acts should be associated by men with the most exclusive of all types of institution. It is only because we are so accustomed to this—taking churches for granted, even when we reject them—that we do not see how odd they really are: how curious it is that men do not set up exclusive and mutually hostile clubs full of rules and regulations to enjoy the light of the sun in particular times and fashions, but do persistently set up such exclusives clubs full of rules and regulations, so to enjoy the free Spirit of God.

When we look into history we see the life of the Spirit, even from its crudest beginnings, closely associated with two movements. First with the tendency to organize it in communities or churches, living under special sanctions and rules. Next, with the tendency of its greatest, most arresting personalities either to revolt from these organisms or to reform, rekindle them from within. So that the institutional life of religion persists through or in spite of its own constant tendency to stiffen and lose fervour, and the secessions, protests, or renewals which are occasioned by its greatest sons. Thus our Lord protested against Jewish formalism; many Catholic mystics, and afterwards the best of the Protestant reformers, against Roman formalism; George Fox against one type of Protestant formalism; the Oxford movement against another. This constant antagonism of church and prophet, of institutional authority and individual vision, is not only true of Christianity but of all great historical faiths. In the middle ages Kabir and Nanak, and in our own times the leaders of the Brahmo Samaj, break away from and denounce ceremonial Hinduism: again and again the great Sufis have led reforms within Islam. That which we are now concerned to discover is the necessity underlying this conflict: the extent in which the institution on one hand serves the spiritual life, and on the other cramps or opposes its free development. It is a truism that all such institutions tend to degenerate, to become mechanical, and to tyrannize. Are they then, in spite of these adverse characters, to be looked on as essential, inevitable, or merely desirable expressions of the spiritual life in man; or can this spiritual life flourish in pure freedom?

This question, often put in the crucial form, "Did Jesus Christ intend to form a Church?" is well worth asking. Indeed, it is of great pressing importance to those who now have the spiritual reconstruction of society at heart. It means, in practice: can men best be saved, regenerated, one by one, by their direct responses to the action of the Spirit; or, is the life of the Spirit best found and actualized through submission to tradition and contacts with other men—that is, in a group or church? And if in a group or church, what should the character of this society be? But we shall make no real movement towards solving this problem, unless we abandon both the standpoint of authority, and that of naïve religious individualism; and consent to look at it as a part of the general problem of human society, in the light of history, of psychology, and of ethics.

I think we may say without exaggeration that the general modern judgment—not, of course, the clerical or orthodox judgment—is adverse to institutionalism; at least as it now exists. In spite of the enormous improvement which would certainly be visible, were we to compare the average ecclesiastical attitude and average Church service in this country with those of a hundred years ago, the sense that religion involves submission to the rules and discipline of a closed society—that definite spiritual gains are attached to spiritual incorporation—that church-going, formal and corporate worship, is a normal and necessary part of the routine of a good life: all this has certainly ceased to be general amongst us. If we include the whole population, and not the pious fraction in our view, this is true both of so-called Catholic and so-called Protestant countries. Professor Pratt has lately described 80 per cent. of the population of the United States as being "unchurched"; and all who worked among our soldiers at the front were struck by the paradox of the immense amount of natural religion existing among them, combined with almost total alienation from religious institutions. Those, too, who study and care for the spiritual life seem most often to conceive it in the terms of William James's well-known definition of religion as "the feelings, acts and experiences of individual men in their solitude, so far as they apprehend themselves to stand in relation to whatever they may consider the Divine."[1]

Such a life of the Spirit—and the majority of educated men would probably accept this description of it—seems little if at all conditioned by Church membership. It speaks in secret to its Father in secret; and private devotion and self-discipline seem to be all it needs. Yet looking at history, we see that this conception, this completeness of emphasis on first-hand solitary seeking, this one-by-one achievement of Eternity, has not in fact proved truly fruitful in the past. Where it seems so to be fruitful, the solitude is illusory. Each great regenerator and revealer of Reality, each God-intoxicated soul achieving transcendence, owes something to its predecessors and contemporaries.² All great spiritual achievement, like all great artistic achievement, however spontaneous it may seem to be, however much the fruit of a personal love and vision, is firmly rooted in the racial past. If fulfills rather than destroys; and unless its free movement towards novelty, fresh levels of pure experience, be thus balanced by the stability which is given us by our hoarded traditions and formed habits, it will degenerate into eccentricity and fail of its full effect. Although nothing but first-hand discovery of and response to spiritual values is in the end of any use to us, that discovery and that response are never quite such a single-handed affair as we like to suppose. Memory and environment, natural and cultural, play their part. And the next most natural and fruitful movement after such a personal discovery of abiding Reality, such a transfiguration of life, is always back towards our fellow-men; to learn more from them, to unite with them, to help them,—anyhow to reaffirm our solidarity with them. The great men and women of the Spirit, then, either use their new power and joy to restore existing institutions to fuller vitality, as did the successive regenerators of the monastic life, such as St. Bernard and St. Teresa and many Sufi saints; or they form new groups, new organisms which they can animate, as did St. Paul, St. Francis, Kabir, Fox, Wesley, Booth. One and all, they feel that the full robust life of the Spirit demands some incarnation, some place in history and social outlet, and also some fixed discipline and tradition.

In fact, not only the history of the soul, but that of all full human achievement, as studied in great creative personalities, shows us that such achievement has always two sides. (1) There is the solitary vision or revelation, and personal work in accordance with that vision. The religious man's direct experience of God and his effort to correspond with it; the artist's lonely and intense apprehension of beauty, and hard translation of it; the poet's dream and its difficult expression in speech; the philosopher's intuition of reality, hammered into thought. These are personal immediate experiences, and no human soul will reach its full stature unless it can have the measure of freedom and withdrawal which they demand. But (2) there are the social and historical contacts which are made by all these creative types with the past and with the present; all the big rich thick stream of human history and effort, giving them, however little they may recognize it, the very initial concepts with which they go to their special contact with reality, and which colour it; supporting them and demanding from them again their contribution to the racial treasury, and to the present too. Thus the artist, as, well as his solitary hours of contemplation and effort, ought to have his times alike of humble study of the past and of intercourse with other living artists; and great and enduring art forms more often arise within a school, than in complete independence of tradition. It seems, then, that the advocates of corporate and personal religion are both, in a measure, right: and that once again a middle path, avoiding both extremes of simplification, keeps nearest to the facts of life. We have no reason for supposing that these principles, which history shows us, have ceased to be operative: or that we can secure the best kind of spiritual progress for the race by breaking with the past and the institutions in which it is conserved. Institutions are in some sort needful if life's balance between stability and novelty, and our links with history and our fellow-men, are to be preserved; and if we are to achieve such a fullness both of individual and of corporate life on highest levels as history and psychology recommend to us.

The question of this institutional side of religion and what we should demand from it falls into two parts, which will best be treated separately. First, that which concerns the character and usefulness of the group-organization or society: the Church. Secondly, that which relates to its peculiar practices: the Cult. We must enquire under each head what are their necessary characters, their essential gifts to the soul, and what their dangers and limitations.

First, then, the Church. What does a Church really do for the God-desiring individual; the soul that wants to live a full, complete and real life, which has "felt in its solitude" the presence and compulsion of Eternal Reality under one or other of the forms of religious experience?

I think we can say that the Church or institution gives to its loyal members:—

- (1) Group-consciousness.
- (2) Religious union, not only with its contemporaries but with the race, that is with history. This we may regard as an extension into the past—and so an enrichment—of that group-consciousness.
- (3) Discipline; and with discipline a sort of spiritual grit, which carries our fluctuating souls past and over the inevitably recurring periods of slackness, and corrects subjectivism.
- (4) It gives Culture, handing on the discoveries of the saints.

In so far as the free-lance gets any of these four things, he gets them ultimately, though indirectly, from some institutional source.

On the other hand the institution, since it represents the element of stability in life, does not give, and must not be expected to give, direct spiritual experience; or any onward push towards novelty, freshness of discovery and interpretation in the spiritual sphere. Its dangers and limitations will abide in a certain dislike of such freshness of discovery; the tendency to exalt the corporate and stable and discount the mobile and individual. Its natural instinct will be for exclusivism, the club-idea, conservatism and cosiness; it will, if left to itself, revel in the middle-aged atmosphere and exhibit the middle-aged point of view.

We can now consider these points in greater detail: and first that of the religious group-consciousness which a church should give its members. This is of a special kind. It is axiomatic that group-organization of some sort is a necessity of human life. History showed us the tendency of all spiritual movements to embody themselves, if not in churches at least in some group-form; the paradox of each successive revolt from a narrow or decadent institutionalism forming a group in its turn, or perishing when its first fervour died. But this social impulse, these spontaneous group-formations of master and disciples, valuable though they may be, do not fully exhibit all that is meant or done by a church. True, the Church is or should be at each moment of its career such a living spiritual society or household of faith. It is, essentially, a community of persons, who have or should have a common sentiment—belief in, and reverence for, their God—and a common defined aim, the furtherance of the spiritual life under the special religious sanctions which they accept. But every sect, every religious order or guild, every class-meeting, might claim this much; yet none of these can claim to be a church.

A church is far more than this. In so far as it is truly alive, it is a real organism, as distinguished from a crowd or collection of persons with a common purpose. It exhibits on the religious plane the ruling characters of such organized life: that is to say, the development of tradition and complex habits, the differentiation of function, the docility to leadership, the conservation of values, or carrying forward of the past into the present. It is, like the State, embodied history; and as such lives with its own life, a life transcending and embracing that of the individual souls of which it is built. And here, in its combined social and historic character, lie the sources alike of its enormous importance for human life and of its inevitable defects.

THE LIFE OF THE SPIRIT AND THE LIFE OF TO-DAY

Professor McDougall, in his discussion of national groups,[3] has laid down the conditions which are necessary to the development of such a true organic group life as is seen in a living church. These are: first, continuity of existence, involving the development of a body of traditions, customs and practices—that is, for religion, a Cultus. Next, an authoritative organization through which custom and belief can be transmitted—that is, a Hierarchy, order of ministers, or its equivalent. Third, a conscious common interest, belief, or idea—Creed. Last, the existence of antagonistic groups or conditions, developing loyalty or keenness. These characters—continuity, authority, common belief and loyalty—which are shown, as he says, in their completeness in a patriot army, are I think no less marked features of a living spiritual society. Plain examples are the primitive Christian communities, the great religious orders in their flourishing time, the Society of Friends. They are on the whole more fully evident in the Catholic than in the Protestant type of church. But I think that we may look upon them, in some form or another, as essential to any institutional framework which shall really help the spiritual life in man.

We find ourselves, then, committed to the picture of a church or spiritual institution which is in essence Liturgic, Ecclesiastical, Dogmatic, and Militant, as best fulfilling the requirements of group psychology. Four decidedly indigestible morsels for the modern mind. Yet, group-feeling demands common expression if it is to be lifted from notion to fact. Discipline requires some authority, and some devotion to it. Culture involves a tradition handed on. And these, we said, were the chief gifts which the institution had to give to its members. We may therefore keep them in mind, as representing actual values, and warning us that neither history nor psychology encourages the belief that an amiable fluidity serves the highest purposes of life. Some common practice and custom, keeping the individual in line with the main tendencies of the group, providing rails on which the instinctive life can run and machinery by which fruitful suggestions can be spread. Some real discipline and humbling submission to rule. Some traditional and theological standard. Some missionary effort and enthusiasm. For these four things we must find place in any incorporation of the spiritual life which is to have its full effect upon the souls of men. And as a matter of fact, the periodical revolts against churches and ecclesiasticism, are never against societies in which all these characteristics are still alive; but against those which retain and exaggerate formal tradition and authority, whilst they have lost zest and identity of aim.

A real Church has therefore something to give to, and something to demand from each of its members, and there is a genuine loss for man in being unchurched. Because it endures through a perpetual process of discarding and renewal, those members will share the richness and experience of a spiritual life far exceeding their own time-span; a truth which is enshrined in the beautiful conception of the Communion of Saints. They enter a group consciousness which reinforces their own in the extent to which they surrender to it; which surrounds them with favourable suggestions and gives the precision of habit to their instinct for Eternity. The special atmosphere, the hoarded beauty, the evocative yet often archaic symbolism, of a Gothic Cathedral, with its constant reminiscences of past civilizations and old levels of culture, its broken fragments and abandoned altars, its conservation of eternal truths—the intimate union in it of the sublime and homely, the successive and abiding aspects of reality—make it the most fitting of all images of the Church, regarded as the spiritual institution of humanity. And the perhaps undue conservatism commonly associated with Cathedral circles represents too the chief reproach which can be brought against churches—their tendency to preserve stability at the expense of novelty, to crystallize, to cling to habits and customs which no longer serve a useful end. In this a church is like a home; where old bits of furniture have a way of hanging on, and old habits, sometimes absurd, endure. Yet both the home and the church can give something which is nowhere else obtainable by us, and represent values which it is perilous to ignore. When once the historical character of reality is fully grasped by us, we see that some such organization through which achieved values are conserved and carried forward, useful habits are learned and practised, the direct intuitions of genius, the prophet's revelation of reality are interpreted and handed on, is essential to the spiritual continuity of the race; and that definite churchmanship of some sort, or its equivalent, must be a factor in the spiritual reconstruction of society. As, other things being equal, a baby benefits enormously by being born within the social framework rather than in the illusory freedom of "pure" nature; so the growth of the soul is, or should be, helped and not hindered by the nurture it receives from the religious society in which it is born. Only indeed by attachment, open or virtual, through life or through literature, to some such group can the new soul link itself with history, and so participate in the hoarded spiritual values of humanity. Thus even a general survey of life inclines us at least to some appreciation of the principle laid down by Baron von Hügel in "Eternal Life"—namely, that "souls who live an heroic spiritual life *within* great religious traditions and institutions, attain to a rare volume and vividness of religious insight, conviction and reality"[4]—seldom within reach of the contemplative, however ardent, who walks by himself.

History has given one reason for this; psychology gives another. These souls, living it is true with intensity their own life towards God, share and are bathed in the group consciousness of their church; as members of a family, distinct in temperament, share and are modified by the group consciousness of the home. The mental process of the individual is profoundly affected when he thus thinks and acts as a member of a group. Suggestibility is then enormously increased; and we know how much suggestion means to us. Moreover, suggestions emanating from the group always take priority of those of the outside world: for man is a gregarious animal, intensely sensitive to the mentality of the herd.[5] The Mind of the Church is therefore a real thing. The individual easily takes colour from it and the tradition it embodies, tends to imitate his fellow-members: and each such deed and thought is a step taken in the formation of habit, and leaves him other than he was before.

To say this is not to discredit church-membership as placing us at the mercy of emotional suggestion, reducing spontaneity to custom, and lessening the energy and responsibility of the individual soul towards God. On the contrary, right group suggestion reinforces, stimulates, does not stultify such individual action. If the prayerful attitude of my fellow worshippers helps me to pray better, surely it is a very mean kind of conceit on my part which would prompt me to despise their help, and refuse to acknowledge Creative Spirit acting on me through other men? It is one of the most beautiful features of a real and living corporate religion, that within it ordinary people at all levels help each other to be a little more supernatural than would have been alone. I do not now speak of individuals possessing special zeal and special aptitude; though, as the lives of the Saints assure us, even the best of these fluctuate, and need social support at times. Anyhow such persons of special spiritual aptitude, as life is now, are as rare as persons of special aptitude in other walks of life. But that which we seek for the life of to-day and of the future, is such a planning of it as shall give all men their spiritual chance. And it is abundantly clear upon all levels of life, that men are chiefly formed and changed by the power of suggestion, sympathy and imitation; and only reach full development when assembled in groups, giving full opportunity for the benevolent action of these forces. So too in the life of the Spirit, incorporation plays a part which nothing can replace. Goodness and devotion are more easily caught than taught; by association in groups, holy and strong souls—both living and dead—make their full gift to society, weak, undeveloped, and arrogant souls receive that of which they are in need. On this point we may agree with a great ecclesiastical scholar of our own day that "the more the educated and intellectual partake with sympathy of heart in the ordinary devotions and pious practices of the poor, the higher will they rise in the religion of the Spirit."[6]

Yet this family life of the ideal religious institution, with its reasonable and bracing discipline, its gift of shelter, its care for tradition, its habit-formation and group consciousness—all this is given, as we may as well acknowledge, at the price which is exacted by all family life; namely, mutual accommodation and sacrifice, place made for the childish, the dull, the slow, and the aged, a toning-down of the somewhat imperious demands of the entirely efficient and clear-minded, a tolerance of imperfection. Thus for these efficient and clear-minded members there is always, in the church as in the family, a perpetual opportunity of humility, self-effacement, gentle acceptance; of exerting that love which must be joined to power and a sound mind if the full life of the Spirit is to be lived. In the realm of the supernatural this is a solid gain; though not a gain which we are very quick to appreciate in our vigorous youth. Did we look upon the religious institution not as an end in itself, but simply as fulfilling the function of a home—giving shelter and nurture, opportunity of loyalty and mutual service on one hand, conserving stability and good custom on the other—then, we should better appreciate its gifts to us, and be more merciful to its necessary defects. We should be tolerant to its inevitable conservatism, its tendency to encourage dependence and obedience to distrust individual initiative. We should no longer expect it to provide or specially to approve novelty and freedom, to be in the van of life's forward thrust. For this we must go not to the institution, which is the vehicle of history; but to the adventurous, forward moving soul, which is the vehicle of progress—to the prophet, not to the priest. These two great figures, the Keeper and the Revealer, which are prominent in every historical religion, represent the two halves of the fully-lived spiritual life. The progress of man depends both on conserving and on exploring: and any full incorporation of that life which will serve man's spiritual interests now, must find place for both.

Such an application of the institutional idea to present needs is required, in fact, to fulfil at least four primary conditions:—

- (1) It must give a social life that shall develop group consciousness in respect of our eternal interests and responsibilities: using for this real discipline, and the influences of liturgy and creed.
- (2) Yet it must not so standardize and socialize this life as to leave no room for personal freedom in the realm of Spirit: for those "experiences of men in their solitude" which form the very heart of religion.
- (3) It must not be so ring-fenced, so exclusive, so wholly conditioned by the past, that the voice of the future, that is of the prophet giving fresh expression to eternal truths, cannot clearly be heard in it; not only from within its own borders but also from outside. But
- (4) On the other hand, it must not be so contemptuous of the past and its priceless symbols that it breaks with tradition, and so loses that very element of stability which it is its special province to preserve.

I go on now to the second aspect of institutional religion: Cultus.

We at once make the transition from Church to Cultus, when we ask ourselves: how does, how can, the Church as an organized and enduring society do its special work of creating an atmosphere and imparting a secret? How is the traditional deposit of spiritual experience handed on, the individual drawn into the stream of spiritual history and held there? Remember, the Church exists to foster and hand on, not merely the moral life, the life of this-world perfection; but the spiritual life in all its mystery and splendour—the life of more than this-world perfection, the poetry of goodness, the life that aims at God. And this, not only in elect souls, which might conceivably make and keep direct contacts without her help, but in greater or less degree in the mass of men, who *do* need help. How is this done? The answer can only be, that it is mostly done through symbolic acts, and by means of suggestion and imitation.

All organized churches find themselves committed sooner or later to an organized cultus. It may be rudimentary. It may reach a high pitch of æsthetic and symbolic perfection. But even the successive rebels against dead ceremony are found as a rule to invent some ceremony in their turn. They learn by experience the truth that men most easily form religious habits and tend, to have religious experiences when they are assembled in groups, and caused to perform the same acts. This is so because as we have already seen, the human psyche is plastic to the suggestions made to it; and this suggestibility is greatly increased when it is living a gregarious life as a member of a united congregation or flock, and is engaged in performing corporate acts. The soldiers' drill is essential to the solidarity of the army, and the religious service in some form is—apart from all other considerations—essential to the solidarity of the Church.

We need not be afraid to acknowledge that from the point of view of the psychologist one prime reason of the value and need of religious ceremonies abides in this corporate suggestibility of man: or that one of their chief works is the production in him of mobility of the threshold, and hence of spiritual awareness of a generalized kind. As the modern mother whispers beneficent suggestions into the ear of her sleeping child[7] so the Church takes her children at their moment of least resistance, and suggests to them all that she desires them to be. It is interesting to note how perfectly adapted the rituals of historic Christianity are to this end, of provoking the emergence of the intuitive mind and securing a state of maximum suggestibility. The more complex and solemn the ritual, the more archaic and universal the symbols it employs, so much the more powerful—for those natures able to yield to it—the suggestion becomes. Music, rhythmic chanting, symbolic gesture, the solemn periods of recited prayer, are all contributory to this, effect In churches of the Catholic type every object that meets the eye, every scent, every attitude that we are encouraged to assume, gives us a push in the same direction if we let it do its rightful work. For other temperaments the collective, deliberate, and really ceremonial silence of the Quakers—the hush of the waiting mind, the unforced attitude of expectation, the abstraction from visual image—works to the same end. In either case, the aim is the production of a special group-consciousness; the reinforcing of languid or undeveloped individual feeling and aptitude by the suggestion of the crowd. This, and its result, is seen of course in its crudest form in revivalism: and on higher levels, in such elaborate dramatic ceremonies as those which are a feature of the Catholic celebrations of Holy Week. But the nice warm devotional feeling with which what is called a good congregation finishes the singing of a favourite hymn belongs to the same order of phenomena. The rhythmic phrases—not as a rule very full of meaning or intellectual appeal —exercise a slightly hypnotic effect on the analyzing surface-mind; and induce a condition of suggestibility open to all the influences of the place and of our fellow worshippers. The authorized translation of Ephesians v. 19: "*speaking to yourselves* in psalms and hymns and spiritual songs," whatever we may think of its accuracy does as it stands describe one of the chief functions of religious services of the "hearty congregational" sort. We do speak to ourselves—our deeper, and more plastic selves—in our psalms and hymns; so too in the common recitation, especially the chanting, of a creed. We administer through these rhythmic affirmations, so long as we sing them with intention, a powerful suggestion to ourselves and every one else within reach. We gather up in them—or should do—the whole tendency of our worship and aspiration, and in the very form in which it can most easily sink in. This lays a considerable responsibility on those who choose psalms and hymns for congregational singing; for these can as easily be the instruments of fanatical melancholy and devitalizing, as of charitable life-giving and constructive ideas.

In saying all this I do not seek to discredit religious ceremony; either of the naïve or of the sophisticated type. On the contrary, I think that in effecting this change in our mental tone and colour, in prompting this emergence of a mood which, in the mass of men, is commonly suppressed, these ceremonies do their true work. They should stimulate and give social expression to that mood of adoration which is the very heart of religion; helping those who cannot be devotional alone to participate in the common devotional feeling. If, then, we desire to receive the gifts which corporate worship can most certainly make to us, we ought to yield ourselves without resistance or criticism to its influence; as we yield ourselves to the influence of a great work of art. That influence is able to tune us up, at least to a fleeting awareness of spiritual reality; and each such emergence of transcendental feeling is to the good. It is true that the objects which immediately evoke this feeling will only be symbolic; but after all, our very best conceptions of God are bound to be that. We do not, or should not, demand scientific truth of them. Their business is rather to give us poetry, a concrete artistic intuition of reality, and to place us in the mood of poetry. The great thing is, that by these corporate liturgic practices and surrenders, we can prevent that terrible freezing up of the deep wells of our being which so easily comes to those who must lead an exacting material or intellectual life. We keep ourselves supple; the spiritual faculties are within reach, and susceptible to education.

Organized ceremonial religion insists upon it, that at least for a certain time each day or week we shall attend to the things of the Spirit. It offers us its suggestions, and shuts off as well as it can conflicting suggestions: though, human as we are, the mere appearance of our neighbours is often enough to bring these in. Nothing is more certain than this: first that we shall never know the spiritual world unless we give ourselves the chance of attending to it, clear a space for it in our busy lives; and next, that it will not produce its real effect in us, unless it penetrates below the conscious surface into the deeps of the instinctive mind, and moulds this in accordance with the regnant idea. If we are to receive the gifts of the cultus, we on our part must bring to it at the very least what we bring to all great works of art that speak to us: that is to say, attention, surrender, sympathetic emotion. Otherwise, like all other works of art, it will remain external to us. Much of the perfectly sincere denunciation and dislike of religious ceremony which now finds frequent utterance comes from those who have failed thus to do their share. They are like the hasty critics who dismiss some great work of art because it is not representative, or historically accurate; and so entirely miss the æsthetic values which it was created to impart.

Consider a picture of the Madonna. Minds at different levels may find in this pure representation, Bible history, theology, æsthetic satisfaction, spiritual truth. The peasant may see in it the portrait of the Mother of God, the critic a phase in artistic evolution; whilst the mystic may pass through it to new contacts with the Spirit of life. We shall receive according to the measure of what we bring. Now consider the parallel case of some great dramatic liturgy, rich with the meanings which history has poured into it. Take, as an example which every one can examine for themselves, the Roman Mass. Different levels of mind will find here magic, theology, deep mystery, the commemoration under archaic symbols of an event. But above and beyond all these, they can find the solemn incorporated emotion, of the Christian Church, and a liturgic recapitulation of the movement of the human soul towards fullness of life: through confession and reconciliation to adoration and intercession—that is, to charity—and thence to direct communion with and feeding on the Divine World.

To the mind which refuses to yield to it, to move with its movement, but remains in critical isolation, the Mass like all other ceremonies will seem external, dead, unreal; lacking in religious content. But if we do give ourselves completely and unselfconsciously to the movement of such a ceremony, at the end of it we may not have learnt anything, but we have lived something. And when we remember that no experience of our devotional life is lost, surely we may regard it as worth while to submit ourselves to an experience by which, if only for a few minutes, we are thus lifted to richer levels of life and brought into touch with higher values? We have indeed only to observe the enrichment of life so often produced in those who thus dwell meekly and without inner conflict in the symbolic world of ceremonial religion, and accept its discipline and its gifts, to be led at least to a humble suspension of judgment as to its value. A whole world of spiritual experience separates the humble little church mouse rising at six every morning to attend a service which she believes to be pleasing to a personal God, from the philosopher who meditates on the Absolute in a comfortable armchair; and no one will feel much doubt as to which side the advantage lies.

Here we approach the next point. The cultus, with its liturgy and its discipline, exists for and promotes the repetition of acts which are primarily the expression of man's instinct for God; and by these—or any other repeated acts—our ductile instinctive life is given a definite trend. We know from Semon's researches[8] that the performance of any given act by a living creature influences all future performances of similar acts. That is to say, memory combines with each fresh stimulus to control our reaction to it. "In the case of living organisms," says Bertrand Russell, "practically everything that is distinctive both of their physical and mental behaviour is bound up with this persistent influence of the past": and most actions and responses "can only be brought under causal laws by including past occurrences in the history of the organism as part of the causes of the present response."[9] The phenomena of apperception, in fact, form only one aspect of a general law. As that which we have perceived conditions what we can now perceive, so that which we have done conditions what we shall do. It therefore appears that in spite of angry youthful revolts or mature sophistications, early religious training, and especially repeated religious *acts*, are likely to influence the whole of our future lives. Though all they meant to us seems dead or unreal, they have retreated to the dark background of consciousness and there live on. The tendency which they have given persists; we never get away from them. A church may often seem to lose her children, as human parents do; but in spite of themselves they retain her invisible seal, and are her children still. In nearly all conversions in middle life, or dramatic returns from scepticism to traditional belief, a large, part is undoubtedly played by forgotten childish memories and early religious discipline, surging up and contributing their part to the self's new apprehensions of Reality.

If, then, the cultus did nothing else, it would do these two highly important things. It would influence our whole present attitude by its suggestions, and our whole future attitude through unconscious memory of the acts which it demands. But it does more than this. It has as perhaps its greatest function the providing of a concrete artistic expression for our spiritual perceptions, adorations and desires. It links the visible with the invisible, by translating transcendent fact into symbolic and even sensuous terms. And for this reason men, having bodies no less surely than spirits, can never afford wholly to dispense with it. Hasty transcendentalists often forget this; and set us spiritual standards to which the race, so long as it is anchored to this planet and to the physical order, cannot conform.

A convert from agnosticism with whom I was acquainted, was once receiving religious instruction from a devout and simple-minded nun. They were discussing the story of the Annunciation, which presented some difficulties to her. At last she said to the nun, "Well, anyhow, I suppose that one is not obliged to believe that the Blessed Virgin was visited by a solid angel, dressed in a white robe?" To this the nun replied doubtfully, "No, dear, perhaps not. But still, you know, he would have to wear *something*."

Now here, as it seems to me, we have a great theological truth in a few words. The elusive contacts and subtle realities of the world of spirit have got to wear something, if we are to grasp them at all. Moreover, if the mass of men are to grasp them ever so little, they must wear something which is easily recognized by the human eye and human heart; more, by the primitive, half-conscious folk-soul existing in each one of us, stirring in the depths and reaching out in its own way towards God. It is a delicate matter to discuss religious symbols. They are like our intimate friends: though at the bottom of our hearts we may know that they are only human, we hate other people to tell us so. And, even as the love of human beings in its most perfect state passes beyond its immediate object, is transfigured, and merged in the nature of all love; so too, the devotion which a purely symbolic figure calls forth from the ardently religious nature— whether this figure be the divine Krishna of Hinduism, the Buddhist's Mother of Mercy, the Sūfi's Beloved, or those objects of traditional Christian piety which are familiar to all of us—this devotion too passes beyond its immediate goal and the relative truth there embodied, and is eternalized. It is characteristic of the primitive mind that it finds a difficulty about universals, and is most at home with particulars. The success of Christianity as a world-religion largely abides in the way in which it meets this need. It is notorious that the person of Jesus, rather than the Absolute God, is the object of average Protestant devotion. So too the Catholic peasant may find it easier to approach God through and in his special saint, or even a special local form of the Madonna. This is the inevitable corollary of the psychic level at which he lives; and to speak contemptuously of his "superstition" is wholly beside the point. Other great faiths have been compelled by experience to meet need of a particular object on which the primitive religious consciousness can fasten itself: conspicuous examples being the development within Buddhism of the cult of the Great Mother, and within pore Brahminism of Krishna worship. Wherever it may be destined to end, here it is that the life of the Spirit begins; emerging very gently from our simplest human impulses and needs. Yet, since the Universal, the Idea, is manifested in each such particular, we need not refuse to allow that the mass of men do thus enjoy—in a way that their psychic level makes natural to them—their own measure of communion with the Creative Spirit of God; and already live according to their measure a spiritual life.

These objects of religious cultus, then, and the whole symbolic faith-world which is built up of them, with its angels and demons, its sharply defined heaven and hell, the Divine personifications which embody certain attributes of God for us, the purity and gentleness of the Mother, the simplicity and infinite possibility of the Child, the divine self-giving of the Cross;—more, the Lamb, the Blood and the Fire of the revivalists, the oil and water, bread and wine, of a finished Sacramentalism—all these may be regarded as the vestures placed by man, at one stage or another of his progress, on the freely-given but ineffable spiritual fact. Like other clothes, they have now become closely identified with that which wears them. And we strip them off at our own peril: for this proceeding, grateful as it may be to our intellects, may leave us face to face with a mystery which we dare not look at, and cannot grasp.

So, cultus has done a mighty thing for humanity, in evolving and conserving the system of symbols through which the Infinite and Eternal can be in some measure expressed. The history of these symbols goes back, as we now know, to the infancy of the race, and forward to the last productions of the religious imagination; all of which bear the image of our past They are like coins, varying in beauty, and often of slight intrinsic value; but of enormous importance for our spiritual currency, because accepted as the representatives of a real wealth. In its symbols, the cultus preserves all the past levels of religious response achieved by the race; weaving them into the fabric of religion, and carrying them forward into the present. All the instinctive movements of the primitive mind; its fear of the invisible, its self-subjection, its trust in ritual acts, amulets, spells, sacrifices, its tendency to localize Deity in certain places or shrines, to buy off the unknown, to set up magicians and mediators, are represented in it. Its function is racial more than individual. It is the art-work of the folk-soul in the religious sphere. Here man's inveterate creative faculty seizes on the raw material given him by religious-intuition, and constructs from it significant shapes. We misunderstand, then, the whole character of religious symbolism if we either demand rationality from it, or try to adapt its imagery to the lucid and probably mistaken conclusions of the sophisticated, modern mind.

We are learning to recognize these primitive and racial elements in popular religion, and to endure their presence with tolerance; because they are necessary, and match a level of mental life which is still active in the race. This more primitive life emerges to dominate all crowds—where the collective mental level is inevitably lower than that of the best individuals immersed in it—and still conditions many of our beliefs and deeds. There is the propitiatory attitude to unseen Divine powers; which the primitive mind, in defiance of theology, insists on regarding as somehow hostile to us and wanting to be bought off. There is the whole idea and apparatus of sacrifice; even though no more than the big apples and vegetable marrows of the harvest festival be involved in it. There is the continued belief in a Deity who can and should be persuaded to change the weather, or who punishes those who offend Him by famine, earthquake and pestilence. Vestigial relics of all these phases can still be discovered in the Book of Common Prayer. There is further the undying vogue of the religious amulet. There is the purely magical efficacy which some churches attribute to their sacraments, rites, shrines, liturgic formulæ and religious objects; others, to the texts of their scriptures.[10] These things, and others like them, are not only significant survivals from the past. They also represent the religious side of something that continues active in us at present. Since, then, it should clearly be the object of all spiritual endeavor to win the whole man and not only his reason for God, speaking to his instincts in language that they understand, we should not too hurriedly despise or denounce these things. Far better that our primitive emotions, with their vast store of potential energy, should be won for spiritual interests on the only terms which they can grasp, than that they should be left to spend themselves on lower objects.

If therefore the spiritual or the regenerate life is not likely to prosper without some incorporation in institutions, some definite link with the past, it seems also likely to need for its full working-out and propaganda the symbols and liturgy of a cultus. Here again, the right path will be that of fulfilment, not of destruction; a deeper investigation of the full meaning of cultus, the values it conserves and the needs it must meet, a clearer and humbler understanding of our human limitations. We must also clearly realize as makers of the future, that as the Church has its special dangers of conservatism, cosiness, intolerance, a checking of initiative, the domestic tendency to enclose itself and shirk reality; so the cultus has also its special dangers, of which the chief are perhaps formalism, magic, and spiritual sloth. Receiving and conserving as it does all the successive deposits of racial experience, it is the very home of magic: of the archaic tendency to attribute words and deeds, special power to a priestly caste, and to make of itself the essential mediator between Creative Spirit and the soul. Further, using perpetually as it does and must symbols of the most archaic sort, directly appealing to the latent primitive in each of us, it offers us a perpetual temptation to fall back into something below our best possible. The impulsive mind is inevitably conservative; always at the mercy of memorized images. Hence its delighted self-yielding to traditional symbols, its uncritical emotionalism, its easy slip-back into traditional and even archaic and self-contradictory beliefs: the way in which it pops out and enjoys itself at a service of the hearty congregational sort, or may even lead its unresisting owner to the revivalists' penitent-bench.

But on the other hand, Creative Spirit is not merely conservative. The Lord and Giver of Life presses forward, and perpetually brings novelty to birth; and in so far as we are dedicated to Him, we must not make an unconditional surrender to psychic indolence, or to the pull-back of the religious past. We may not, as Christians, accept easy emotions in the place of heroic and difficult actualizations: make external religion an excuse for dodging reality, immerse ourselves in an exquisite dream, or tolerate any real conflict between old cultus and actual living faith. A most delicate discrimination is therefore demanded from us; the striking of a balance between the rightful conservatism of the cultus and the rightful independence of the soul. Yet, this is not to justify even in the most advanced a wholesale iconoclasm. Time after time, experience has proved that the attempt to approach God "without means," though it may seem to describe the rare and sacred moments of the personal life of the Spirit, is beyond the power of the mass of men; and even those who do achieve it are, as it were, most often supported from behind by religious history and the religious culture of their day. I do not think it can be doubted that the right use of cultus does-increase religious sensitiveness. Therefore here the difficult task of the future must be to preserve and carry forward its essential elements, all the symbolic significance, all the incorporated emotion, which make it one of man's greatest works of art; whilst eliminating those features which are, in the bad sense, conventional and no longer answer to experience or communicate life.

Were we truly reasonable human beings, we should perhaps provide openly and as a matter of course within the Christian frame widely different types of ceremonial religion, suited to different levels of mind and different developments of the religious consciousness. To some extent this is already done: traditionalism and liberalism, sacramentalism, revivalism, quietism, have each their existing cults. But these varying types of church now appear as competitors, too often hostile; not as the complementary and graded expressions of one life, each having truth in the relative though none in the absolute sense. Did we more openly acknowledge the character of that life, the historic Churches would no longer invite the sophisticated to play down to their own primitive fantasies; to sing meaningless hymns and recite vindictive psalms, or lull themselves by the recitation of litany or rosary which, admirable as the instruments of suggestion, are inadequate expressions of the awakened spiritual life. On the one hand, they would not require the simple to express their corporate religious feeling in Elizabethan English or Patristic Latin; on the other, expect the educated to accept at face-value symbols of which the unreal character is patent to them. Nor would they represent these activities as possessing absolute value in themselves.

To join in simplicity and without criticism in the common worship, humbly receiving its good influences, is one thing. This is like the drill of the loyal soldier; welding him to his neighbours, giving him the corporate spirit and forming in him the habits he needs. But to stop short at that drill, and tell the individual that drill is the essence of his life and all his duty, is another thing altogether. It confuses means and end; destroys the balance between liberty and law. If the religious institution is to do its real work in furthering the life of the Spirit, it must introduce a more rich variety into its methods; and thus educate souls of every type not only to be members of the group but also to grow up to the full richness of the personal life. It must offer them—as indeed Catholicism does to some extent already—both easy emotion and difficult mystery; both dramatic ceremony and ceremonial silence. It must also give to them all its hoarded knowledge of the inner life of prayer and contemplation, of the remaking of the moral nature on supernatural levels: all the gold that there is in the deposit of faith. And it must not be afraid to impart that knowledge in modern terms which all can understand. All this it can and will do if its members sufficiently desire it: which means, if those who care intensely for the life of the Spirit accept their corporate responsibilities. In the last resort, criticism of the Church, of Christian institutionalism, is really criticism of ourselves. Were we more spiritually alive, our spiritual homes would be the real nesting places of new life. That which the Church is to us is the result of all that we bring to, and ask from, history: the impact of our present and its past.

---

1. William James: "The Varieties of Religious Experience," p. 31.
2. On this point compare Von Hügel: "Essays and Addresses on the Philosophy of Religion," pp. 230 et seq.
3. W. McDougall: "The Group Mind," Cap. 3.
4. Von Hügel "Eternal Life," p. 377.
5. Cf. Trotter: "Instincts of the Herd in Peace and War."
6. Dom Cuthbert Butler in the "Hibbert Journal," 1906, p. 502.
7. Baudouin: "Suggestion and Auto-Suggestion," Cap. VII.
8. Cf. R. Semon: "Die Mneme."
9. Bertrand Russell: "The Analysis of Mind," p. 78.
10. A quaint example of this occurred in a recent revival, where the exclamation "We believe in the Word of God from cover to cover, Alleluia!" received the fervent reply, "And the covers too!"

CHAPTER VI

THE LIFE OF THE SPIRIT IN THE INDIVIDUAL

In the last three chapters we have been concerned, almost exclusively, with those facts of psychic life and growth, those instruments and mechanizations, which bear upon or condition our spiritual life. But these wanderings in the soul's workshops, and these analyses of the forces that play on it, give us far too cold or too technical a view of that richly various and dynamic thing, the real regenerated life. I wish now to come out of the workshop, and try to see this spiritual life as the individual man may and should achieve it, from another angle of approach.

What are we to regard as the heart of spirituality? When we have eliminated the accidental characters with which varying traditions have endowed it, what is it that still so definitely distinguishes its possessor from the best, most moral citizen or devoted altruist? Why do the Christian saint, Indian *rishi,* Buddhist *arhat,* Moslem *Sūfi,* all seem to us at bottom men of one race, living under different sanctions one life, witnessing to one fact? This life, which they show in its various perfections, includes it is true the ethical life, but cannot be equated with it. Wherein do its differentia consist? We are dealing with the most subtle of realities and have only the help of crude words, developed for other purposes than this. But surely we come near to the truth, as history and experience show it to us, when we say again that the spiritual life in all its manifestations from smallest beginnings to unearthly triumph is simply the life that means God in all His richness, immanent and transcendent:

THE LIFE OF THE SPIRIT AND THE LIFE OF TO-DAY

the whole response to the Eternal and Abiding of which any one man is capable, expressed in and through his this-world life. It requires then an objective vision or certitude, something to aim at; and also a total integration of the self, its dedication to that aim. Both terms, vision and response, are essential to it.

This definition may seem at first sight rather dull. It suggests little of that poignant and unearthly beauty, that heroism, that immense attraction, which really belong to the spiritual life. Here indeed we are dealing with poetry in action: and we need not words but music to describe it as it really is. Yet all the forms, all the various beauties and achievements of this life of the Spirit, can be resumed as the reactions of different temperaments to the one abiding and inexhaustibly satisfying Object of their love. It is the answer made by the whole supple, plastic self, rational and instinctive, active and contemplative, to any or all of those objective experiences of religion which we considered in the first chapter; whether of an encompassing and transcendent Reality, of a Divine Companionship or of Immanent Spirit. Such a response we must believe to be itself divinely actuated. Fully made, it is found on the one hand to call forth the most heroic, most beautiful, most tender qualities in human nature; all that we call holiness, the transfiguration of mere ethics by a supernatural loveliness, breathing another air, satisfying another standard, than those of the temporal world. And on the other hand, this response of the self is repaid by a new sensitiveness and receptivity, a new influx of power. To use theological language, will is answered by grace: and as the will's dedication rises towards completeness the more fully does new life flow in. Therefore it is plain that the smallest and humblest beginning of such a life in ourselves—and this inquiry is useless unless it be made to speak to our own condition—will entail not merely an addition to life, but for us too a change in our whole scale of values, a self-dedication. For that which we are here shown as a possible human achievement is not a life of comfortable piety, or the enjoyment of the delicious sensations of the armchair mystic. We are offered, it is true, a new dower of life; access to the full possibilities of human nature. But only upon terms, and these terms include new obligations in respect of that life; compelling us, as it appears, to perpetual hard and difficult choices, a perpetual refusal to sink back into the next-best, to slide along a gentle incline. The spiritual life is not lived upon the heavenly hearth-rug, within safe distance from the Fire of Love. It demands, indeed, very often things so hard that seen from the hearth-rug they seem to us superhuman: immensely generous compassion, forbearance, forgiveness, gentleness, radiant purity, self-forgetting zeal. It means a complete conquest of life's perennial tendency to lag behind the best possible; willing acceptance of hardship and pain. And if we ask how this can be, what it is that makes possible such enhancement of human will and of human courage, the only answer seems to be that of the Johannine Christ: that it does consist in a more abundant life.

In the second chapter of this book, we looked at the gradual unfolding of that life in its great historical representatives; and we found its general line of development to lead through disillusion with the merely physical to conversion to the spiritual, and thence by way of hard moral conflicts and their resolution to a unification of character, a full integration of the active and contemplative sides of life; resulting in fresh power, and a complete dedication, to work within the new order and for the new ideals. There was something of the penitent, something of the contemplative, and something of the apostle in every man or woman who thus grew to their full stature and realized all their latent possibilities. But above all there was a fortitude, an all-round power of tackling existence, which comes from complete indifference to personal suffering or personal success. And further, psychology showed us, that those workings and readjustments which we saw preparing this life of the Spirit, were in line with those which prepare us for fullness of life on other levels: that is to say the harnessing of the impulsive nature to the purposes chosen by consciousness, the resolving of conflicts, the unification of the whole personality about one's dominant interest. These readjustments were helped by the deliberate acceptance of the useful suggestions of religion, the education of the foreconscious, the formation of habits of charity and prayer.

The greatest and most real of living writers on this subject, Baron von Hügel, has given us another definition of the personal spiritual life which may fruitfully be compared with this. It must and shall, he says, exhibit rightful contact with and renunciation of the Particular and Fleeting; and with this ever seeks and finds the Eternal—deepening and incarnating within its own experience this "transcendent Otherness."[1] Nothing which we are likely to achieve can go beyond this profound saying. We see how many rich elements are contained in it: effort and growth, a temper both social and ascetic, a demand for and a receiving of power. True, to some extent it restates the position at which we arrived in the first chapter: but we now wish to examine more thoroughly into that position and discover its practical applications. Let us then begin by unpacking it, and examining its chief characters one by one.

If we do this, we find that it demands of us:—

- (1) Rightful contact with the Particular and Fleeting. That is, a willing acceptance of all this-world tasks, obligations, relations, and joys; in fact, the Active Life of Becoming in its completeness.
- (2) But also, a certain renunciation of that Particular and Fleeting. A refusal to get everything out of it that we can for ourselves, to be possessive, or attribute to it absolute worth. This involves a sense of detachment or asceticism; of further destiny and obligation for the soul than complete earthly happiness or here-and-now success.
- (3) And with this ever—not merely in hours of devotion—to seek and find the Eternal; penetrating our wholesome this-world action through and through with the very spirit of contemplation.
- (4) Thus deepening and incarnating—bringing in, giving body to, and in some sense exhibiting by means of our own growing and changing experience—that transcendent Otherness, the fact of the Life of the Spirit in the here-and-now.

The full life of the Spirit, then, is once more declared to be active, contemplative, ascetic and apostolic; though nowadays we express these abiding human dispositions in other and less formidable terms. If we translate them as work, prayer, self-discipline and social service they do not look quite so bad. But even so, what a tremendous programme to put before the ordinary human creature, and how difficult it looks when thus arranged! That balance to be discovered and held between due contact with this present living world of time, and due renunciation of it. That continual penetration of the time-world with the spirit of Eternity.

But now, in accordance with the ruling idea which has occupied us in this book, let us arrange these four demands in different order. Let us put number three first: "ever seeking and finding the Eternal." Conceive, at least, that we do this really, and in a practical way. Then we discover that, placed as we certainly are in a world of succession, most of the seeking and finding has got to be done there; that the times of pure abstraction in which we touch the non-successive and supersensual must be few. Hence it follows that the first and second demands are at once fully met; for, if we are indeed faithfully seeking and finding the Eternal whilst living—as all sane men and women must do—in closest contact with the Particular and Fleeting, our acceptances and our renunciations will be governed by this higher term of experience. And further, the transcendent Otherness, perpetually envisaged by us as alone giving the world of sense its beauty, reality and value, will be incarnated and expressed by us in this sense-life, and thus ever more completely tasted and known. It will be drawn by us, as best we can, and often at the cost of bitter struggle, into the limitations of humanity; entincturing our attitude and our actions. And in the degree in which we thus appropriate it, it will be given out by us again to other men.

All this, of course, says again that which men have been constantly told by those who sought to redeem them from their confusions, and show them the way to fullness of life. "Seek first the Kingdom of God," said Jesus, "and all the rest shall be added to you." "Love," said St. Augustine, "and *do* what you like"; "Let nothing," says Thomas à Kempis, "be great or high or acceptable to thee but purely God";[2] and Kabir, "Open your eyes of love, and see Him who pervades this world! consider it well, and know that this is your own country."[3] "Our whole teaching," says Boehme, "is nothing else than how man should kindle in himself God's light-world."[4] I do not say that such a presentation of it makes the personal spiritual life any easier: nothing does that. But it does make its central implicit rather clearer, shows us at once its difficulty and its simplicity; since it depends on the consistent subordination of every impulse and every action to one regnant aim and interest—in other words, the unification of the whole self round one centre, the highest conceivable by man. Each of man's behaviour-cycles is always directed towards some end, of which he may or may not be vividly conscious. But in that perfect unification of the self which is characteristic of the life of Spirit, all his behaviour is brought into one stream of purpose, and directed towards one transcendent end. And this simplification alone means for him a release from conflicting wishes, and so a tremendous increase of power.

If then we admit this formula, "ever seeking and finding the Eternal"—which is of course another rendering of Ruysbroeck's "aiming at God"—as the prime character of a spiritual life, the secret of human transcendence; what are the agents by which it is done?

Here, men and women of all times and all religions, who have achieved this fullness of life, agree in their answer: and by this answer we are at once taken away from dry philosophic conceptions and introduced into the very heart of human experience. It is done, they say, on man's part by Love and Prayer: and these, properly understood in their inexhaustible richness, joy, pain, dedication and noble simplicity, cover the whole field of the spiritual life. Without them, that life is impossible; with them, if the self be true to their implications, some measure of it cannot be escaped. I said, Love and Prayer properly understood: not as two movements of emotional piety, but as fundamental human dispositions, as the typical attitude and action which control man's growth into greater reality. Since then they are of such primary importance to us, it will be worth while at this stage to look into them a little more closely.

First, Love: that over-worked and ill-used word, often confused on the one hand with passion and on the other with amiability. If we ask the most fashionable sort of psychologist what love is, he says that it is the impulse urging us towards that end which is the fulfilment of any series of deeds or "behaviour-cycle"; the psychic thread, on which all the apparently separate actions making up that cycle are strung and united. In this sense love need not be fully conscious, reach the level of feeling; but it *must* be an imperative, inward urge. And if we ask those who have known and taught the life of the Spirit, they too say that love is a passionate tendency, an inward vital urge of the soul towards its Source;[5] which impels every living thing to pursue the most profound trend of its being, reaches consciousness in the form of self-giving and of desire, and its only satisfying goal in God. Love is for them much more than its emotional manifestations. It is "the ultimate cause of the true activities of all active things"—no less. This definition, which I take as a matter of fact from St. Thomas Aquinas,[6] would be agreeable to the most modern psychologist; he might give the hidden steersman of the psyche in its perpetual movement towards novelty a less beautiful and significant name. "This indwelling Love," says Plotinus, "is no other than the Spirit which, as we are told, walks with every being, the affection dominant in each several nature. It implants the characteristic desire; the particular soul, strained towards its own natural objects, brings forth its own Love, the guiding spirit realizing its worth and the quality of its being."[7]

Does not all this suggest to us once more, that at whatever level it be experienced, the psychic craving, the urgent spirit within us pressing out to life, is always *one;* and that the sublimation of this vital craving, its direction to God, is the essence of regeneration? There, in our instinctive nature—which, as we know, makes us the kind of animal we are—abides that power of loving which is, really, the power of living; the cause of our actions, the controlling factor in our perceptions, the force pressing us into any given type of experience, turning aside for no obstacles but stimulated by them to a greater vigour. Each level of the universe makes solicitations to this power: the worlds of sense, of thought, of beauty, and of action. According to the degree of our development, the trend of the conscious will, is our response; and according to that response will be our life. "The world to which a man turns himself," says Boehme, "and in which he produces fruit, the same is lord in him, and this world becomes manifest in him."[8]

From all this it becomes clear what the love of God is; and what St. Augustine meant when he said that all virtue—and virtue after all means power not goodness—lay in the right ordering of love, the conscious orientation of desire. Christians, on the authority of their Master, declare that such love of God requires all that they have, not only of feeling, but also of intellect and of power; since He is to be loved with heart and mind and strength. Thought and action on highest levels are involved in it, for it means, not religious emotionalism, but the unflickering orientation of the whole self towards Him, ever seeking and finding the Eternal; the linking up of all behaviour on that string, so that the apparently hard and always heroic choices which are demanded, are made at last because they are inevitable. It is true that this dominant interest will give to our lives a special emotional colour and a special kind of happiness; but in this, as in the best, deepest, richest human love, such feeling-tone and such happiness—though in some natures of great beauty and intensity—are only to be looked upon as secondary characters, and never to be aimed at.

When St. Teresa said that the real object of the spiritual marriage was "the incessant production of work, work,"[9] I have no doubt that many of her nuns were disconcerted; especially the type of ease-loving conservatives whom she and her intimates were accustomed to refer to as the pussy-cats. But in this direct application to religious experience of St. Thomas' doctrine of love, she set up an ideal of the spiritual life which is as valid at the present day in the entanglements of our social order, as it was in the enclosed convents of sixteenth-century Spain. Love, we said, is the cause of action. It urges and directs our behaviour, conscious and involuntary, towards an end. The mother is irresistibly impelled to act towards her child's welfare, the ambitious man towards success, the artist towards expression of his vision. All these are examples of behaviour, love-driven towards ends. And religious experience discloses to us a greater more inclusive end, and this vital power of love as capable of being used on the highest levels, regenerated, directed to eternal interests;

subordinating behaviour, inspiring suffering, unifying the whole self and its activities, mobilizing them for this transcendental achievement. This generous love, to go back to the quotation from Baron von Hügel which opened our inquiry, will indeed cause the behaviour it controls to exhibit both rightful contact with and renunciation of the particular and fleeting; because in and through this series of linked deeds it is uniting with itself all human activities, and in and through them is seeking and finding its eternal end. So, in that rightful bringing-in of novelty which is the business of the fully living soul, the most powerful agent is love, understood as the controlling factor of behaviour, the sublimation and union of will and desire. "Let love," says Boehme, "be the life of thy nature. It killeth thee not, but quickeneth thee according to its life, and then thou livest, yet not to thy own will but to its will: for thy will becometh its will, and then thou art dead to thyself but alive to God."[10] There is the true, solid and for us most fruitful doctrine of divine union, unconnected with any rapture, trance, ecstasy or abnormal state of mind: a union organic, conscious, and dynamic with the Creative Spirit of Life.

If we now go on to ask how, specially, we shall achieve this union in such degree as is possible to each one of us; the answer must be, that it will be done by Prayer. If the seeking of the Eternal is actuated by love, the finding of it is achieved through prayer. Prayer, in fact—understood as a life or state, not an act or an asking—is the beginning, middle and end of all that we are now considering. As the social self can only be developed by contact with society, so the spiritual self can only be developed by contact with the spiritual world. And such humble yet ardent contact with the spiritual world—opening up to its suggestions our impulses, our reveries, our feelings, our most secret dispositions as well as our mere thoughts- is the essence of prayer, understood in its widest sense. No more than surrender or love can prayer be reduced to "one act." Those who seek to sublimate it into "pure" contemplation are as limited at one end of the scale, as those who reduce it to articulate petition are at the other. It contains in itself a rich variety of human reactions and experiences. It opens the door upon an unwalled world, in which the self truly lives and therefore makes widely various responses to its infinitely varying stimuli. Into that world the self takes, or should take, its special needs, aptitudes and longings, and matches them against its apprehension of Eternal Truth. In this meeting of the human heart with all that it can apprehend of Reality, not adoration alone but unbounded contrition, not humble dependence alone but joy, peace and power, not rapture alone but mysterious darkness, must be woven into the fabric of love. In this world the soul may sometimes wander as if in pastures, sometimes is poised breathless and intent. Sometimes it is fed by beauty, sometimes by most difficult truth, and experiences the extremes of riches and destitution, darkness and light. "It is not," says Plotinus, "by crushing the Divine into a unity but by displaying its exuberance, as the Supreme Himself has displayed it, that we show knowledge of the might of God."[11]

Thus, by that instinctive and warmly devoted direction of its behaviour which is love, and that willed attention to and communion with the spiritual world which is prayer, all the powers of the self are united and turned towards the seeking and finding of the Eternal. It is by complete obedience to this exacting love, doing difficult and unselfish things, giving up easy and comfortable things—in fact by living, living hard on the highest levels —that men more and more deeply feel, experience, and enter into their spiritual life. This is a fact which must seem rather awkward to those who put forward pathological explanations of it. And on the other hand it is only by constant contacts with and recourse to the energizing life of Spirit, that this hard vocation can be fulfilled. Such a power of reference to Reality, of transcending the world of succession and its values, can be cultivated by us; and this education of our inborn aptitude is a chief function of the discipline of prayer. True, it is only in times of recollection or of great emotion that this profound contact is fully present to consciousness. Yet, once fully achieved and its obligations accepted by us, it continues as a grave melody within our busy outward acts: and we must by right direction of our deepest instincts so find and feel the Eternal all the time, if indeed we are to actualize and incarnate it all the time. From this truth of experience, religion has deduced the doctrine of grace, and the general conception of man as able to do nothing of himself. This need hardly surprise us. For equally on the physical plane man can do nothing of himself, if he be cut off from his physical sources of power: from food to eat, and air to breathe. Therefore the fact that his spiritual life too is dependent upon the life-giving atmosphere that penetrates him, and the heavenly food which he receives, makes no fracture in his experience. Thus we are brought back by another path to the fundamental need for him, in some form, of the balanced active and contemplative life.

In spite of this, many people seem to take it for granted that if a man believes in and desires to live a spiritual life, he can live it in utter independence of spiritual food. He believes in God, loves his neighbour, wants to do good, and just goes ahead. The result of this is that the life of the

THE LIFE OF THE SPIRIT AND THE LIFE OF TO-DAY

God-fearing citizen or the Social Christian, as now conceived and practised, is generally the starved life. It leaves no time for the silence, the withdrawal, the quiet attention to the spiritual, which is essential if it is to develop all its powers. Yet the literature of the Spirit is full of warnings on this subject. *Taste* and see that the Lord is sweet. They that wait upon the Lord shall renew their *strength*. In quietness and confidence shall be your *strength*. These are practical statements; addressed, not to specialists but to ordinary men and women, with a normal psycho-physical make-up. They are literally true now, or can be if we choose. They do not involve any peculiar training, or unnatural effort. A sliding scale goes from the simplest prayer-experience of the ordinary man to that complete self-loss and complete self-finding, which is called the transforming union of the saint; and somewhere in this series, every human soul can find a place.

If this balanced life is to be ours, if we are to receive what St. Augustine called the food of the full-grown, to find and feel the Eternal, we must give time and place to it in our lives. I emphasize this, because its realization seems to me to be a desperate modern need; a need exhibited supremely in our languid and ineffectual spirituality, but also felt in the too busy, too entirely active and hurried lives of the artist, the reformer and the teacher. St. John of the Cross says in one of his letters: "What is wanting is not writing or talking—there is more than enough of that—but, silence and action. For silence joined to action produces recollection, and gives the spirit a marvellous strength." Such recollection, such a gathering up of our interior forces and retreat of consciousness to its "ground," is the preparation of all great endeavour, whatever its apparent object may be. Until we realize that it is better, more useful, more productive of strength, to spend, let us say, the odd ten minutes in the morning in feeling and finding the Eternal than in flicking the newspaper—that this will send us off to the day's work properly orientated, gathered together, recollected, and really endowed with new power of dealing with circumstance—we have not begun to live the life of the Spirit, or grasped the practical connection between such a daily discipline and the power of doing our best work, whatever it may be.

I will illustrate this from a living example: that of the Sadhu Sundar Singh. No one, I suppose, who came into personal contact with the Sadhu, doubted that they were in the presence of a person who was living, in the full sense, the spiritual life. Even those who could not accept the symbols in which he described his experience and asked others to share it, acknowledged that there had been worked in him a great transformation;

that the sense of the abiding and eternal went with him everywhere, and flowed out from him, to calm and to correct our feverish lives. He fully satisfies in his own person the demands of Baron von Hügel's definition: both contact with and renunciation of the Particular and Fleeting, seeking and finding of the Eternal, incarnating within his own experience that transcendent Otherness. Now the Sadhu has discovered for himself and practises as the condition of his extraordinary activity, power and endurance, just that balance of life which St. Benedict's rule ordained. He is a wandering missionary, constantly undertaking great journeys, enduring hardship and danger, and practising the absolute poverty of St. Francis. He is perfectly healthy, strong, extraordinarily attractive, full of power. But this power he is careful to nourish. His irreducible minimum is two hours spent in meditation and wordless communication with God at the beginning of each day. He prefers three or four hours when work permits; and a long period of prayer and meditation always precedes his public address. If forced to curtail or hurry these hours of prayer, he feels restless and unhappy, and his efficiency is reduced. "Prayer," he says, "is as important as breathing; and we never say we have no time to breathe."[12]

All this has been explained away by critics of the muscular Christian sort, who say that the Sadhu's Christianity is of a typically Eastern kind. But this is simply not true. It were much better to acknowledge that we, more and more, are tending to develop a typically Western kind of Christianity, marked by the Western emphasis on doing and Western contempt for being; and that if we go sufficiently far on this path we shall find ourselves cut off from our source. The Sadhu's Christianity is fully Christian; that is to say, it is whole and complete. The power in which he does his works is that in which St. Paul carried through his heroic missionary career, St. Benedict formed a spiritual family that transformed European culture, Wesley made the world his parish, Elizabeth Fry faced the Newgate criminals. It is idle to talk of the revival of a personal spiritual life among ourselves, or of a spiritual regeneration of society—for this can only come through the individual remaking of each of its members—unless we are willing, at the sacrifice of some personal convenience, to make a place and time for these acts of recollection; this willing and loving—and even more fruitful, the more willing and loving—communion with, response to Reality, to God. It is true that a fully lived spiritual life involves far more than this. But this is the only condition on which it will exist at all.

Love then, which is a willed tendency to God; prayer, which is willed communion with and experience of Him; are the two prime essentials in the personal life of the Spirit. They represent, of course, only our side of it and our obligation. This love is the outflowing response to another inflowing love, and this prayer the appropriation of a transcendental energy and grace. As the "German Theology" reminds us, "I cannot do the work without God, and God may not or will not without me."[13] And by these acts alone, faithfully carried through, all their costly demands fulfilled, all their gifts and applications accepted without resistance and applied to each aspect of life, human nature can grow up to its full stature, and obtain access to all its sources of power.

Yet this personal inward life of love and prayer shall not be too solitary. As it needs links with cultus and so with the lives of its fellows, it also needs links with history and so with the living past. These links are chiefly made by the individual through his reading; and such reading—such access to humanity's hoarded culture and experience—has always been declared alike by Christian and non-Christian asceticism to be one of the proper helps of the spiritual life. Though Höffding perhaps exaggerates when he reminds us that mediæval art always depicts the saints as deeply absorbed in their books, and suggests that such brooding study directly induces contemplative states,[14] yet it is true that the soul gains greatly from such communion with, and meek learning from, its cultural background. Ever more and more as it advances, it will discover within that background the records of those very experiences which it must now so poignantly relive; and which seem to it, as his own experience seems to every lover, unique. There it can find, without any betrayal of its secret, the wholesome assurance of its own normality; standards of comparison; companionship, alike in its hours of penitence, of light, and of deprivation. Yet such fruitful communion with the past is not the privilege of an aristocratic culture. It is seen in its perfection in many simple Christians who have found in the Bible all the spiritual food they need. The great literature of the Spirit tells its secrets to those alone who thus meet it on its own ground. Not only the works of Thomas à Kempis, of Ruysbroeck, or of St. Teresa, but also the Biblical writers—and especially, perhaps, the Psalms and the Gospels—are read wholly anew by us at each stage of our advance. Comparative study of Hindu and Moslem writers proves that this is equally true of the great literatures of other faiths.[15] Beginners may find in all these infinite stimulus, interest, and beauty. But to the mature soul they become road-books, of which experience proves the astonishing exactitude; giving it descriptions which it can recognize and directions that it needs, and constituting a steady check upon individualism.

Now let us look at the emergence of this life which we have been considering, and at the typical path which it will or may follow, in an ordinary man or woman of our own day. Not a saint or genius, reaching heroic levels; but a member of that solid wholesome spiritual population which ought to fill the streets of the City of God. We noticed when we were studying its appearance in history, that often this life begins in a sort of restlessness, a feeling that there is something more in existence, some absolute meaning, some more searching obligation, that we have not reached. This dissatisfaction, this uncertainty and hunger, may show itself in many different forms. It may speak first to the intellect, to the moral nature, to the social conscience, even to the artistic faculty; or, directly, to the heart. Anyhow, its abiding quality is a sense of contraction, of limitation; a feeling of something more that we could stretch out to, and achieve, and be. Its impulsion is always in one direction; to a finding of some wider and more enduring reality, some objective for the self's life and love. It is a seeking of the Eternal, in some form. I allow that thanks to the fog in which we live muffled, such a first seeking, and above all such a finding of the Eternal is not for us a very easy thing. The sense of quest, of disillusion, of something lacking, is more common among modern men than its resolution in discovery. Nevertheless the quest does mean that there is a solution: and that those who are persevering must find it in the end. The world into which our desire is truly turned, is somehow revealed to us. The revelation, always partial and relative, is of course conditioned by our capacity, the character of our longing and the experiences of our past. In spiritual matters we behold that which we are: here following, on higher levels, the laws which govern æsthetic apprehension.

So, dissatisfied with its world-view and realizing that it is incomplete, the self seeks at first hand, though not always with clear consciousness of its nature, the Reality which is the object of religion. When it finds this Reality, the discovery, however partial, is for it the overwhelming revelation of an objective Fact; and it is swept by a love and awe which it did not know itself to possess. And now it sees; dimly, yet in a sufficiently disconcerting way, the Pattern in the Mount; the rich complex of existence as it were transmuted, full of charity and beauty, governed by another series of adjustments. Life looks different to it. As Fox said, "Creation gives out another smell than before."[16] There is only one thing more disconcerting than this, and that is seeing the pattern actualized in a fellow human being: living face to face with human sanctity, in its great simplicity and supernatural love, joy, peace. For, when we glimpse Eternal Beauty in the universe, we can say with the hero of "Callista," "It is beyond me!" But, when we see it transfiguring human character, we know that it is not beyond the power of the race. It is here, to be had. Its existence as a form of life creates a standard, and lays an obligation on us all.

Suppose then that the self, urged by this new pressure, accepts the obligation and measures itself by the standard. It then becomes apparent that this Fact which it sought for and has seen is not merely added to its old universe, as in mediæval pictures Paradise with its circles over-arches the earth. This Reality is all-penetrating and has transfigured each aspect of the self's old world. It now has a new and most exacting scale of values, which demand from it a new series of adjustments; ask it—and with authority—to change its life.

What next? The next thing, probably, is that the self finds itself in rather a tight place. It is wedged into a physical order that makes innumerable calls on it, and innumerable suggestions to it: which has for years monopolized its field of consciousness and set up habits of response to its claims. It has to make some kind of a break with this order, or at least with its many attachments thereto; and stretch to the wider span demanded by the new and larger world. And further, it is in possession of a complex psychic life, containing many insubordinate elements, many awkward bequests from a primitive past. That psychic life has just received the powerful and direct suggestion of the Spirit; and for the moment, it is subdued to that suggestion. But soon it begins to experience the inevitable conflict between old habits, and new demands—between a life lived in the particular and in the universal spirit—and only through complete resolution of that conflict will it develop its full power. So the self quickly realizes that the theologian's war between Nature and Grace is a picturesque way of stating a real situation; and further that the demand of all religions for a change of heart—that is, of the deep instinctive nature—is the first condition of a spiritual life. And hence, that its hands are fairly full. It is true that an immense joy and hope come with it to this business of tackling imperfection, of adjusting itself to the newly found centre of life. It knows that it is committed to the forward movement of a Power, which may be slow but which nothing can gainsay. Nevertheless the first thing that power demands from it is courage; and the next an unremitting vigorous effort. It will never again be able to sink back cosily into its racial past. Consciousness of disharmony and incompleteness now brings the obligation to mend the disharmony and achieve a fresh synthesis.

This is felt with a special sharpness in the moral life, where the irreconcilable demands of natural self-interest and of Spirit assume their most intractable shape. Old habits and paths of discharge which have almost become automatic must now, it seems, be abandoned. New paths, in spite of resistances, must be made. Thus it is that temptation, hard conflict, and bewildering perplexities usher in the life of the Spirit. These are largely the results of our biological past continuing into our fluctuating half-made present; and they point towards a psychic stability, an inner unity we have not yet attained.

This realization of ourselves as we truly are—emerging with difficulty from our animal origin, tinctured through and through with the self-regarding tendencies and habits it has imprinted on us—this realization or self-knowledge, is Humility; the only soil in which the spiritual life can germinate. And modern man with his great horizons, his ever clearer vision of his own close kinship with life's origin, his small place in the time-stream, in the universe, in God's hand, the relative character of his best knowledge and achievement, is surely everywhere being persuaded to this royal virtue. Recognition of this his true creaturely status, with its obligations—the only process of pain and struggle needed if the demands of generous love are ever to be fulfilled in him and his many-levelled nature is to be purified and harmonized and develop all its powers—this is Repentance. He shows not only his sincerity, but his manliness and courage by his acceptance of all that such repentance entails on him; for the healthy soul, like the healthy body, welcomes some trial and roughness and is well able to bear the pains of education. Psychologists regard such an education, harmonizing the rational or ideal with the instinctive life—the change of heart which leaves the whole self working together without inner conflict towards one objective—as the very condition of a full and healthy life. But it can only be achieved in its perfection by the complete surrender of heart and mind to a third term, transcending alike the impulsive and the rational. The life of the Spirit in its supreme authority, and its identification with the highest interests of the race, does this: harnessing man's fiery energies to the service of the Light.

Therefore, in the rich, new life on which the self enters, one strand must be that of repentance, catharsis, self-conquest; a complete contrition which is the earnest of complete generosity, uncalculated response. And, dealing as we are now with average human nature, we can safely say that the need for such ever-renewed self-scrutiny and self-purgation will never in this life be left behind. For sin is a fact, though a fact which we do not understand; and now it appears and must evermore remain an offence against love, hostile to this intense new attraction, and marring the self's willed tendency towards it.

The next strand we may perhaps call that of Recollection: for the recognizing and the cure of imperfection depends on the compensating search for the Perfect and its enthronement as the supreme object of our thought and love. The self, then, soon begins to feel a strong impulse to some type of inward withdrawal and concentration, some kind of prayer; though it may not use this name or recognize the character of its mood. As it yields to this strange new drawing, such recollection grows easier. It finds that there is a veritable inner world, not merely of phantasy, but of profound heart-searching experience; where the soul is in touch with another order of realities and knows itself to be an inheritor of Eternal Life. Here unique things happen. A power is at work, and new apprehensions are born. And now for the first time the self discovers itself to be striking a balance between this inner and the outer life, and in its own small way—but still, most fruitfully—enriching action with the fruits of contemplation. If it will give to the learning of this new art—to the disciplining and refining of this affective thought—even a fraction of the diligence which it gives to the learning of a new game, it will find itself repaid by a progressive purity of vision, a progressive sense of assurance, an ever-increasing delicacy of moral discrimination and demand. Psychologists, as we have seen, divide men into introverts and extroverts; but as a matter of fact we must regard both these extreme types as defective. A whole man should be supple in his reactions both to the inner and to the outer world.

The third strand in the life of the Spirit, for this normal self which we are considering; must be the disposition of complete Surrender. More and more advancing in this inner life, it will feel the imperative attraction of Reality, of God; and it must respond to this attraction with all the courage and generosity of which it is capable. I am trying to use the simplest and the most general language, and to avoid emotional imagery: though it is here, in telling of this perpetually renewed act of self-giving and dedication, that spiritual writers most often have recourse to the language of the heart. It is indeed in a spirit of intensest and humble adoration that generous souls yield themselves to the drawing of that mysterious Beauty and unchanging Love, with all that it entails. But the form which the impulse to surrender takes will vary with the psychic make-up of the individual. To some it will come as a sense of vocation, a making-over of the will to the purposes of the Kingdom; a type of consecration which may not be overtly religious, but may be concerned with the self-forgetting quest of social excellence, of beauty, or of truth. By some it will be felt as an illumination of the mind, which now discerns once for all true values, and accepting these, must uphold and strive for them in the teeth of all opportunism. By some—and these are the most blessed—as a breaking and remaking of the heart. Whatever the form it takes, the extent in which the self experiences the peace, joy and power of living at the level of Spirit will depend on the completeness and singlemindedness of this, its supreme act of self-simplification. Any reserves, anything in its make-up which sets up resistances—and this means generally any form of egotism—will mar the harmony of the process. And on the other hand, such a real simplification of the self's life as is here demanded—uniting on one object, the intellect, will and feeling too often split among contradictory attractions—is itself productive of inner harmony and increased power: productive too of that noble endurance which counts no pain too much in the service of Reality.

Here then we come to the fact, valid for every level of spiritual life, which lies behind all the declarations concerning surrender, self-loss, dying to live, dedication, made by writers on this theme. All involve a relaxing of tension, letting ourselves go without reluctance in the direction in which we are most profoundly drawn; a cessation of our struggles with the tide, our kicks against the pricks that spur us on. The inward aim of the self is towards unification with a larger life; a mergence with Reality which it may describe under various contradictory symbols, or may not be able to describe at all, but which it feels to be the fulfilment of existence. It has learnt—though this knowledge may not have passed beyond the stage of feeling—that the universe is one simple texture, in which all things have their explanation and their place. Combing out the confusions which enmesh it, losing its sham and separate life and finding its true life there, it will know what to love and how to act. The goal of this process, which has been called entrance into the freedom of the Will of God, is the state described by the writer of the "German Theology" when he said "I would fain be to the Eternal Goodness what his own hand is to a man."[17] For such a declaration not only means a willed and skilful working for God, a practical siding with Perfection, becoming its living tool, but also close union with, and sharing of, the vital energy of the spiritual order: a feeding on and using of its power, its very life blood; complete docility to its inward direction, abolition of separate desire. The surrender is therefore made not in order that we may become limp pietists, but in order that we may receive more energy and do better work: by a humble self-subjection more perfectly helping forward the thrust of the Spirit and the primal human business of incarnating the Eternal here and now. Its justification is in the arduous but untiring, various but harmonious, activities that flow from it: the enhancement of life which it entails. It gives us access to our real sources of power; that we may take from them and, spending generously, be energized anew.

So the cord on which those events which make up the personal life of the Spirit are to be strung is completed, and we see that it consists of four strands. Two are dispositions of the self; Penitence and Surrender. Two are activities; inward Recollection and outward Work. All four make stern demands on its fortitude and goodwill. And each gives strength to the rest: for they are not to be regarded as separate and successive states, a discrete series through which we must pass one by one, leaving penitence behind us when we reach surrendered love; but as the variable yet enduring and inseparable aspects of one rich life, phases in one complete and vital effort to respond more and more closely to Reality.

Nothing, perhaps, is less monotonous than the personal life of the Spirit. In its humility and joyous love, its adoration and its industry, it may find self-expression in any one of the countless activities of the world of time. It is both romantic and austere, both adventurous and holy. Full of fluctuation and unearthly colour, it yet has its dark patches as well as its light. Since perfect proof of the supersensual is beyond the span of human consciousness, the element of risk can never be eliminated: we are obliged in the end to trust the universe and live by faith. Therefore the awakened soul must often suffer perplexity, share to the utmost the stress and anguish of the physical order; and, chained as it is to a consciousness accustomed to respond to that order, must still be content with flashes of understanding and willing to bear long periods of destitution when the light is veiled.

The further it advances the more bitter will these periods of destitution seem to it. It is not from the real men and women of the Spirit that we hear soft things about the comfort of faith. For the true life of faith gives everything worth having and takes everything worth offering: with unrelenting blows it welds the self into the stuff of the universe, subduing it to the universal purpose, doing away with the flame of separation.

Though joy and inward peace even in desolation are dominant marks of those who have grown up into it, still it offers to none a succession of supersensual delights. The life of the Spirit involves the sublimation of that pleasure-pain rhythm which is characteristic of normal consciousness, and if for it pleasure becomes joy, pain becomes the Cross. Toil, abnegation, sacrifice, are therefore of its essence; but these are not felt as a heavy burden, because they are the expression of love. It entails a willed tension and choice, a noble power of refusal, which are not entirely covered by being "in tune with the Infinite." As our life comes to maturity we discover to our confusion that human ears can pick up from the Infinite many incompatible tunes, but cannot hear the whole symphony. And the melody confided to our care, the one which we alone perhaps can contribute and which taxes our powers to the full, has in it not only the notes of triumph but the notes of pain. The distinctive mark therefore is not happiness but vocation: work demanded and power given, but given only on condition that we spend it and ourselves on others without stint. These propositions, of course, are easily illustrated from history: but we can also illustrate them in our own persons if we choose.

Should we choose this, and should life of the Spirit be achieved by us —and it will only be done through daily discipline and attention to the Spiritual, a sacrifice of comfort to its interests, following up the intuition which sets us on the path—what benefits may we as ordinary men expect it to bring to us and to the community that we serve? It will certainly bring into life new zest and new meaning; a widening of the horizon and consciousness of security; a fresh sense of joys to be had and of work to be done. The real spiritual consciousness is positive and constructive in type: it does not look back on the past sins and mistakes of the individual or of the community, but in its other-world faith and this-world charity is inspired by a forward-moving spirit of hope. Seeking alone the honour of Eternal Beauty, and because of its invulnerable sense of security, it is adventurous. The spiritual man and woman can afford to take desperate chances, and live dangerously in the interests of their ideals; being delivered from the many unreal fears and anxieties which commonly torment us, and knowing the unimportance of possessions and of so-called success. The joy which waits on disinterested love and the confidence which follows surrender, cannot fail them. Moreover, the inward harmony and assurance, the consciousness of access to that Spirit who is in a literal sense "health's eternal spring" means a healing of nervous miseries, and invigoration of the usually ill-treated mind and body, and so an all-round increase in happiness and power.

"The fruit of the Spirit is love, joy, peace, long suffering, gentleness, goodness, faith, meekness, temperance." This, said St. Paul, who knew by experience the worlds of grace and of nature, is what a complete man ought to be like. Compare this picture of an equable and fully harmonized personality with that of a characteristic neurasthenic, a bored sensualist, or an embittered worker, concentrated on the struggle for a material advantage: and consider that the central difference between these types of human success and human failure abides in the presence or absence of a spiritual conception of life. We do not yet know the limits of the upgrowth into power and happiness which complete and practical surrender to this conception can work in us; or what its general triumph might do for the transformation of the world. And it may even be that beyond the joy and renewal which come from self-conquest and unification, a level of spiritual life most certainly open to all who will really work for it; and beyond that deeper insight, more widespreading love, and perfection of adjustment to the here-and-now which we recognize and reverence as the privilege of the pure in heart—beyond all these, it may be that life still reserves for man another secret and another level of consciousness; a closer identification with Reality, such as eye hath not seen, or ear heard.

And note, that this spiritual life which we have here considered is not an aristocratic life. It is a life of which the fundamentals are given by the simplest kinds of traditional piety, and have been exhibited over and over again by the simplest souls. An unconditional self-surrender to the Divine Will, under whatever symbols it may be thought of; for we know that the very crudest of symbols is often strong enough to make a bridge between the heart and the Eternal, and so be a vehicle of the Spirit of Life. A little silence and leisure. A great deal of faithfulness, kindness, and courage. All this is within the reach of anyone who cares enough for it to pay the price.

---

1. This doctrine is fully worked out in the last two sections of "Eternal Life."
2. De Imit. Christi, Bk. II, Cap. 6.
3. "Six Theosophic Points," p. 75.
4. "One Hundred Poems of Kabir," p. 78.
5. Cl. Ruysbroeck: "The Mirror of Eternal Salvation," Cap. VIII
6. "In Librum B. Dionysii de Divinis Nominibus commentaria."
7. Ennead III. 5, 4.
8. Boehme: "Six Theosophic Points," p. 75.
9. "The Interior Castle"; Seventh Habitation, Cap. IV.

10. Boehme; "The Way to Christ," Pt. IV.
11. Ennead II. 9. 9.
12. "Streeter and Appasamy: The Sadhu," pp. 98, 100 et seq., 213.
13. "Theologia Germanica," Cap. III.
14. Höffding, "The Philosophy of Religion," III, B.
15. There are, for instance, several striking instances in the Autobiography of the Maharishi Devendranath Tagore.
16. "Fox's Journal," Vol. I, Cap. 2.
17. "Theologia Germanica," Cap. 10.

CHAPTER VII

THE LIFE OF THE SPIRIT AND EDUCATION

In the past six chapters we have been considering in the main our own position, and how, here in the present, we as adults may actualize and help on the spiritual life in ourselves. But our best hope of giving Spirit its rightful, full expression within the time-world lies in the future. It is towards that, that those who really care must work. Anything which we can do towards persuading into better shape our own deformed characters, compelling our recalcitrant energy into fresh channels, is little in comparison with what might be achieved in the plastic growing psychic life of children did we appreciate our full opportunity and the importance of using it. This is why I propose now to consider one or two points in the relation of education to the spiritual life.

Since it is always well, in a discussion of this kind, to be quite clear about the content of the words with which we deal, I will say at once, that by Education I mean that deliberate adjustment of the whole environment of a growing creature, which surrounds it with the most favourable influences and educes all its powers; giving it the most helpful conditions for its full growth and development. Education should be the complete preparation of the young thing for fullness of life; involving the evolution and the balanced training of all its faculties, bodily, mental and spiritual. It should train and refine senses, instincts, intellect, will and feeling; giving a world-view based on real facts and real values and encouraging active correspondence therewith. Thus the educationist, if he be convinced, as I think most of us must be, that all isn't quite right with the world of mankind, has the priceless opportunity of beginning the remaking of humanity from the right end. In the child he has a little, supple thing, which can be made into a vital, spiritual thing; and nothing again will count so much for it as what happens in these its earliest years. To start life straight is the secret of inward happiness: and to a great extent, the secret of health and power.

That conception of man upon which we have been working, and which regards his psychic life on all its levels as the manifold expressions of one single energy or urge in the depths of his being, a life-force seeking fulfilment, has obvious and important applications in the educational sphere. It indicates that the fundamental business of education is to deal with this urgent and untempered craving, discipline it, and direct it towards interests of permanent value: helping it to establish useful habits, removing obstacles in its path, blocking the side channels down which it might run. Especially is it the task of such education, gradually to disclose to the growing psyche those spiritual correspondences for which the religious man and the idealist must hold that man's spirit was made. Such an education as this has little in common with the mere crude imparting of facts. It represents rather the careful and loving induction of the growing human creature into the rich world of experience; the help we give it in the great business of adjusting itself to reality. It operates by means of the moulding influences of environment, the creation of habit. Suggestion, not statement, is its most potent instrument; and such suggestion begins for good or ill at the very dawn of consciousness. Therefore the child whose infancy is not surrounded by persons of true outlook is handicapped from the start; and the training in this respect of the parents of the future is one of the greatest services we can render to the race.

We are beginning to learn the overwhelming importance of infantile impressions: how a forgotten babyish fear or grief may develop underground, and produce at last an unrecognizable growth poisoning the body and the mind of the adult. But here good is at least as potent as ill. What terror, a hideous sight, an unloving nurture may do for evil; a happy impression, a beautiful sight, a loving nurture will do for good. Moreover, we can bury good seed in the unconscious minds of children and reasonably look forward to the fruit. Babyish prayers, simple hymns, trace whilst the mind is ductile the paths in which feelings shall afterwards tend to flow; and it is only in maturity that we realize our psychological debt to these early and perhaps afterwards abandoned beliefs and deeds. So the veritable education of the Spirit begins at once, in the cradle, and its chief means will be the surroundings within which that childish spirit first develops its little awareness of the universe; the appeals which are made to its instincts, the stimulations of its life of sense. The first factor of this education is the family: the second the society within which that family is formed.

Though we no longer suppose it to possess innate ideas, the baby has most surely innate powers, inclinations and curiosities, and is reaching out in every direction towards life. It is brimming with will power, ready to push hard into experience. The environment in which it is placed and the responses which the outer world makes to it—and these surroundings and responses in the long run are largely of our choosing and making—represent either the helping or thwarting of its tendencies, and the sum total of the directions in which its powers can be exercised and its demands satisfied: the possibilities, in fact, which life puts before it. We, as individuals and as a community, control and form part of this environment. Under the first head, we play by influence or demeanour a certain part in the education of every child whom we meet. Under the second head, by acquiescence in the social order, we accept responsibility for the state of life in which it is born. The child's first intimations of the spiritual must and can only come to it through the incarnation of Spirit in its home and the world that it knows. What, then, are we doing about this? It means that the influences which shape the men and women of the future will be as wholesome and as spiritual as we ourselves are: no more, no less. Tone, atmosphere are the things which really matter; and these are provided by the group-mind, and reflect its spiritual state.

The child's whole educational opportunity is contained in two factors; the personality it brings and the environment it gets. Generations of educationists have disputed their relative importance: but neither party can deny that the most fortunate nature, given wrongful or insufficient nurture, will hardly emerge unharmed. Even great inborn powers atrophy if left unused, and exceptional ability in any direction may easily remain undeveloped if the environment be sufficiently unfavourable: a result too often achieved in the domain of the spiritual life. We must have opportunity and encouragement to try our powers and inclinations, be helped to understand their nature and the way to use them, unless we are to begin again, each one of us, in the Stone Age of the soul. So too, even small powers may be developed to an astonishing degree by suitable surroundings and wise education —witness the results obtained by the expert training of defective children

—and all this is as applicable to the spiritual as to the mental and bodily life. That life is quick to respond to the demands made on it: to take every opportunity of expression that comes its way. If you make the right appeal to any human faculty, that faculty will respond, and begin to grow. Thus it is that the slow quiet pressure of tradition, first in the home and then in the school, shapes the child during his most malleable years. We, therefore, are surely bound to watch and criticize the environment, the tradition, the customs we are instrumental in providing for the infant future: to ask ourselves whether we are *sure* the tradition is right, the conventions we hand on useful, the ideal we hold up complete. The child, whatever his powers, cannot react to something which is not there; he can't digest food that is not given to him, use faculties for which no objective is provided. Hence the great responsibility of our generation, as to providing a complete, balanced environment *now*, a fully-rounded opportunity of response to life physical, mental and spiritual, for the generation preparing to succeed us. Such education as this has been called a preparation for citizenship. But this conception is too narrow, unless the citizenship be that of the City of God; and the adjustments involved be those of the spirit, as well as of the body and the mind.

Herbert Spencer, whom one would hardly accuse of being a spiritual philosopher, was accustomed to group the essentials of a right education under four heads:[1]

- First, he said, we must teach self-preservation in all senses: how to keep the body and the mind healthy and efficient, how to be self-supporting, how to protect oneself against external dangers and encroachments.
- Next, we must train the growing creature in its duties towards the life of the future: parenthood and its responsibilities, understood in the widest sense.
- Thirdly; we must prepare it to take its place in the present as a member of the social order into which it is born.
- Last: we must hand on to it all those refinements of life which the past has given to us—the hoarded culture of the race.

Only if we do these four things thoroughly can we dare to call ourselves educators in the full sense of the word.

Now, turning to the spiritual interests of the child:—and unless we are crass materialists we must believe these interests to exist, and to be paramount—what are we doing to further them in these four fundamental directions? First, does the average good education train our young people in spiritual self-preservation? Does it send them out equipped with the means of living a full and efficient spiritual life? Does it furnish them with a health-giving type of religion; that is, a solid hold on eternal realities, a view of the universe capable of withstanding hostile criticism, of supporting them in times of difficulty and of stress? Secondly, does it give them a spiritual outlook in respect of their racial duties, fit them in due time to be parents of other souls? Does it train them to regard humanity, and their own place in the human life-stream, from this point of view? This point is of special importance, in view of the fact that racial and biological knowledge on lower levels is now so generally in the possession of boys and girls; and is bound to produce a distorted conception of life, unless the spirit be studied by them with at least the same respectful attention that is given to the flesh. Thirdly, what does our education do towards preparing them to solve the problems of social and economic life in a spiritual sense—our only reasonable chance of extracting the next generation from the social muddle in which we are plunged to-day? Last, to what extent do we try to introduce our pupils into a full enjoyment of their spiritual inheritance, the culture and tradition of the past?

I do not deny that there are educators—chiefly perhaps educators of girls—who can give favourable answers to all these questions. But they are exceptional, the proportion of the child population whom they influence is small, and frequently their proceedings are looked upon—not without some justice—as eccentric. If then in all these departments our standard type of education stops short of the spiritual level, are not we self-convicted as at best theoretical believers in the worth and destiny of the human soul?

Consider the facts. Outside the walls of definitely religious institutions—where methods are not always adjusted to the common stuff and needs of contemporary human life—it does not seem to occur to many educationists to give the education of the child's soul the same expert delicate attention so lavishly bestowed on the body and the intellect. By expert delicate attention I do not mean persistent religious instruction; but a skilled and loving care for the growing spirit, inspired by deep conviction and helped by all the psychological knowledge we possess. If we look at the efforts of organized religion we are bound to admit that in thousands of rural parishes, and in many towns too, it is still possible to grow from infancy to old age as a member of church or chapel without once receiving any first-hand teaching on the powers and needs of the soul or the technique of prayer; or obtaining any more help in the great religious difficulties of adolescence than a general invitation to believe, and trust God. Morality—that is to say correctness of response to our neighbour and our temporal surroundings—is often well taught. Spirituality— correctness of response to God and our eternal surroundings—is most often ignored. A peculiar British bashfulness seems to stand in the way of it. It is felt that we show better taste in leaving the essentials of the soul's development to chance, even that such development is not wholly desirable or manly: that the atrophy of one aspect of "man's made-trinity" is best. I have heard one eminent ecclesiastic maintain that regular and punctual attendance at morning service in a mood of non-comprehending loyalty was the best sort of spiritual experience for the average Englishman. Is not that a statement which should make the Christian teachers who are responsible for the average Englishman, feel a little bit uncomfortable about the type which they have produced? I do not suggest that education should encourage a feverish religiosity; but that it ought to produce balanced men and women, whose faculties are fully alert and responsive to all levels of life. As it is, we train Boy Scouts and Girl Guides in the principles of honour and chivalry. Our Bible-classes minister to the hungry spirit much information about the journeys of St. Paul (with maps). But the pupils are seldom invited or assisted to *taste*, and see that the Lord is sweet.

Now this indifference means, of course, that we do not as educators, as controllers of the racial future, really believe in the spiritual foundations of our personality as thoroughly and practically we believe in its mental and physical manifestations. Whatever the philosophy or religion we profess may be, it remains for us in the realm of idea, not in the realm of fact. In practice, we do not aim at the achievement of a spiritual type of consciousness as the crown of human culture. The best that most education does for our children is only what the devil did for Christ. It takes them up to the top of a high mountain and shows them all the kingdoms of this world; the kingdom of history, the kingdom of letters, the kingdom of beauty, the kingdom of science. It is a splendid vision, but unfortunately fugitive: and since the spirit is not fugitive, it demands an objective that is permanent. If we do not give it such an objective, one of two things must happen to it. Either it will be restless and dissatisfied, and throw the whole life out of key; or it will become dormant for lack of use, and so the whole life will be impoverished, its best promise unfulfilled. One line leads to the neurotic, the other to the average sensual man, and I think it will be agreed that modern life produces a good crop of both these kind of defectives.

But if we believe that the permanent objective of the spirit is God—if He be indeed for us the Fountain of Life and the sum of Reality—can we acquiesce in these forms of loss? Surely it ought to be our first aim, to make the sense of His universal presence and transcendent worth, and of the self's responsibility to Him, dominant for the plastic youthful consciousness confided to our care: to introduce that consciousness into a world which is really a theocracy and encourage its aptitude for generous love? If educationists do not view such a proposal with favour, this shows how miserable and distorted our common conception of God has become; and how small a part it really plays in our practical life. Most of us scramble through that practical life, and are prepared to let our children scramble too, without any clear notions of that hygiene of the soul which has been studied for centuries by experts; and few look upon this branch of self-knowledge as something that all men may possess who will submit to education and work for its achievement. Thus we have degenerated from the mediæval standpoint; for then at least the necessity of spiritual education was understood and accepted, and the current psychology was in harmony with it. But now there is little attempt to deepen and enlarge the spiritual faculties, none to encourage their free and natural development in the young, or their application to any richer world of experience than the circle of pious images with which "religious education" generally deals. The result of this is seen in the rawness, shallowness and ignorance which characterize the attitude of many young adults to religion. Their beliefs and their scepticism alike are often the acceptance or rejection of the obsolete. If they be agnostics, the dogmas which they reject are frequently theological caricatures. If they be believers, both their religious conceptions and their prayers are found on investigation still to be of an infantile kind, totally unrelated to the interests and outlook of modern men.

Two facts emerge from the experience of all educationists. The first is, that children are naturally receptive and responsive; the second, that adolescents are naturally idealistic. In both stages, the young human creature is full of interests and curiosities asking to be satisfied, of energies demanding expression; and here, in their budding, thrusting life—for which we, by our choice of surroundings and influence, may provide the objective—is the raw material out of which the spiritual humanity of the future might be made. The child has already within it the living seed wherein all human possibilities are contained; our part is to give the right soil, the shelter, and the watering-can. Spiritual education therefore does not consist in putting into the child something which it has not; but in educing and sublimating that which it has—in establishing habits, fostering a trend of growth which shall serve it well in later years. Already, all the dynamic instincts are present, at least in germ; asking for an outlet. The will and the emotions, ductile as they will never be again, are ready to make full and ungraduated response to any genuine appeal to enthusiasm. The imagination will accept the food we give, if we give it in the right way. What an opportunity! Nowhere else do we come into such direct contact with the plastic stuff of life; never again shall we have at our disposal such a fund of emotional energy.

In the child's dreams and fantasies, in its eager hero-worship—later, in the adolescent's fervid friendships or devoted loyalty to an adored leader—we see the search of the living growing creature for more life and love, for an enduring object of devotion. Do we always manage or even try to give it that enduring object, in a form it can accept? Yet the responsibility of providing such a presentation of belief as shall evoke the spontaneous reactions of faith and love—for no compulsory idealism ever succeeds—is definitely laid on the parent and the teacher. It is in the enthusiastic imitation of a beloved leader that the child or adolescent learns best. Were the spiritual life the most real of facts to us, did we believe in it as we variously believe in athletics, physical science or the arts, surely we should spare no effort to turn to its purposes these priceless qualities of youth? Were the mind's communion with the Spirit of God generally regarded as its natural privilege and therefore the first condition of its happiness and health, the general method and tone of modern education would inevitably differ considerably from that which we usually see: and if the life of the Spirit is to come to fruition, here is one of the points at which reformation must begin. When we look at the ordinary practice of modern "civilized" Europe, we cannot claim that any noticeable proportion of our young people are taught during their docile and impressionable years the nature and discipline of their spiritual faculties, in the open and common-sense way in which they are taught languages, science, music or gymnastics. Yet it is surely a central duty of the educator to deepen and enrich to the fullest extent possible his pupil's apprehension of the universe; and must not all such apprehension move towards the discovery of that universe as a spiritual fact?

Again, in how many schools is the period of religious and idealistic enthusiasm which so commonly occurs in adolescence wisely used, skilfully trained, and made the foundation of an enduring spiritual life? Here is the period in which the relation of master and pupil is or may be most intimate and most fruitful; and can be made to serve the highest interests of life. Yet, no great proportion of those set apart to teach young people seem to realize and use this privilege.

I am aware that much which I am going to advocate will sound fantastic; and that the changes involved may seem at first sight impossible to accomplish. It is true that if these changes are to be useful, they must be gradual. The policy of the "clean sweep" is one which both history and psychology condemn. But it does seem to me a good thing to envisage clearly, if we can, the ideal towards which our changes should lead. A garden city is not Utopia. Still, it is an advance upon the Victorian type of suburb and slum; and we should not have got it if some men had not believed in Utopia, and tried to make a beginning here and now. Already in education some few have tried to make such a beginning and have proved that it is possible if we believe in it enough: for faith can move even that mountainous thing, the British parental mind.

Our task—and I believe our most real hope for the future—is, as we have already allowed, to make the idea of God dominant for the plastic youthful consciousness: and not only this, but to harmonize that conception, first with our teachings about the physical and mental sides of life, and next with the child's own social activities, training body, mind and spirit together that they may take each their part in the development of a whole man, fully responsive to a universe which is at bottom a spiritual fact. Such training to be complete must, as we have seen, begin in the nursery and be given by the atmosphere and opportunities of the home. It will include the instilling of childish habits of prayer and the fostering of simple expressions of reverence, admiration and love. The subconscious knowledge implicit in such practice must form the foundation, and only where it is present will doctrine and principle have any real meaning for the child. Prayer must come before theology, and kindness, tenderness and helpfulness before ethics.

But we have now to consider the child of school age, coming—too often without this, the only adequate preparation—into the teacher's hands. How is he to be dealt with, and the opportunities which he presents used best?

"When I see a right man," said Jacob Boehme, "there I see three worlds standing." Since our aim should be to make "right men" and evoke in them not merely a departmental piety but a robust and intelligent spirituality, we ought to explain in simple ways to these older children something at least of that view of human nature on which our training is based. The religious instruction given in most schools is divided, in varying proportions, between historical or doctrinal teaching and ethical teaching. Now a solid hold both on history and on morals is a great need; but these are only realized in their full importance and enter completely into life when they are seen within the spiritual atmosphere, and already even in childhood, and supremely in youth, this atmosphere can be evoked. It does not seem to occur to most teachers that religion contains anything beyond or within the two departments of historical creed and of morals: that, for instance, the greatest utterances of St. John and St. Paul deal with neither, but with attainable levels of human life, in which a new and fuller kind of experience was offered to mankind. Yet surely they ought at least to attempt to tell their pupils about this. I do not see how Christians at any rate can escape the obligation, or shuffle out of it by saying that they do not know how it can be done. Indeed, all who are not thorough-going materialists must regard the study of the spiritual life as in the truest sense a department of biology; and any account of man which fails to describe it, as incomplete. Where the science of the body is studied, the science of the soul should be studied too. Therefore, in the upper forms at least, the psychology of religious experience in its widest sense, as a normal part of all full human existence, and the connection of that experience with practical life, as it is seen in history, should be taught. If it is done properly it will hold the pupil's interest, for it can be made to appeal to those same mental qualities of wonder, curiosity and exploration which draw so many boys and girls to physical science. But there should be no encouragement of introspection, none of the false mystery or so-called reverence with which these subjects are sometimes surrounded, and above all no spirit of exclusivism.

    The pupil should be led to see his own religion as a part of the universal tendency of life to God. This need not involve any reduction of the claims made on him by his own church or creed; but the emphasis should always be on the likeness rather than the differences of the great religions of the world. Moreover, higher education cannot be regarded as complete unless the mind be furnished with some *rationale* of its own deepest experiences, and a harmony be established between impulse and thought. Advanced pupils should, then, be given a simple and general philosophy of religion, plainly stated in language which relates it with the

THE LIFE OF THE SPIRIT AND THE LIFE OF TO-DAY

current philosophy of life. This is no counsel of perfection. It has been done, and can be done again. It is said of Edward Caird, that he placed his pupils "from the beginning at a point of view whence the life of mankind could be contemplated as one movement, single though infinitely varied, unerring though wandering, significant yet mysterious, secure and self-enriching although tragical. There was a general sense of the spiritual nature of reality and of the rule of mind, though what was meant by spirit or mind was hardly asked. There was a hope and faith that outstripped all save the vaguest understanding but which evoked a glad response that somehow God was immanent in the world and in the history of all mankind, making it sane." And the effect of this teaching on the students was that "they received the doctrine with enthusiasm, and forgot themselves in the sense of their partnership in a universal enterprise."[2] Such teaching as this is a real preparation for citizenship, an introduction to the enduring values of the world.

Every human being, as we know, inevitably tends to emphasize some aspects of that world, and to ignore others: to build up for himself a relative universe. The choices which determine the universe of maturity are often made in youth; then the foundations are laid of that apperceiving mass which is to condition all the man's contacts with reality. We ought, therefore, to show the universe to our young people from such an angle and in such a light, that they tend quite simply and without any objectionable intensity to select, emphasize and be interested in its spiritual aspect. For this purpose we must never try to force our own reading of that universe upon them; but respect on the one hand their often extreme sensitiveness and on the other the infinitely various angles of approach proper to our infinitely various souls. We should place food before them and leave them to browse. Only those who have tried this experiment know what such an enlargement of the horizon and enrichment of knowledge means to the eager, adolescent mind: how prompt is the response to any appeal which we make to its nascent sense of mystery. Yet whole schools of thought on these subjects are cheerfully ignored by the majority of our educationists; hence the unintelligent and indeed babyish view of religion which is harboured by many adults, even of the intellectual class.

Though the spiritual life has its roots in the heart not in the head, and will never be brought about by merely academic knowledge; yet, its beginnings in adolescence are often lost, because young people are completely ignorant of the meaning of their own experiences, and the universal character of those needs and responses which they dimly feel stirring within them. They are too shy to ask, and no one ever tells them about it in a business-like and unembarrassing way. This infant mortality in the spiritual realm ought not to be possible. Experience of God is the greatest of the rights of man, and should not be left to become the casual discovery of the few. Therefore prayer ought to be regarded as a universal human activity, and its nature and difficulties should be taught, but always in the sense of intercourse rather than of mere petition: keeping in mind the doctrine of the mystics that "prayer in itself properly is not else but a devout intent directed unto God."[3] We teach concentration for the purposes of study; but too seldom think of applying it to the purposes of prayer. Yet real prayer is a difficult art; which, like other ways of approaching Perfect Beauty, only discloses its secrets to those who win them by humble training and hard work. Shall we not try to find some method of showing our adolescents their way into this world, lying at our doors and offered to us without money and without price?

Again, many teachers and parents waste the religious instinct and emotional vigour which are often so marked in adolescence, by allowing them to fritter themselves upon symbols which cannot stand against hostile criticism: for instance, some of, the more sentimental and anthropomorphic aspects of Christian devotion. Did we educate those instincts, show the growing creature their meaning, and give them an objective which did not conflict with the objectives of the developing intellect and the will, we should turn their passion into power, and lay the foundations of a real spiritual life. We must remember that a good deal of adolescent emotion is diverted by the conditions of school-life from its obvious and natural objective. This is so much energy set free for other uses. We know how it emerges in hero-worship or in ardent friendships; how it reinforces the social instinct and produces the team-spirit, the intense devotion to the interests of his own gang or group which is rightly prominent in the life of many boys. The teacher has to reckon with this funded energy and enthusiasm, and use it to further the highest interests of the growing child. By this I do not mean that he is to encourage an abnormal or emotional concentration on spiritual things. Most of the impulses of youth are wholesome, and subserve direct ends. Therefore, it is not by taking away love, self-sacrifice, admiration, curiosity, from their natural objects that we shall serve the best interests of spirituality: but, by enlarging the range over which these impulses work—impulses, indeed, which no human object can wholly satisfy, save in a sacramental sense. Two such natural tendencies, specially prominent in childhood, are peculiarly at the disposal of the religious teacher: and should be used by him to the full. It is in the sublimation of the instinct of comradeship that the social and corporate side of the spiritual life takes its rise, and in closest connection with this impulse that all works of charity should be suggested and performed. And on the individual side, all that is best, safest and sweetest in the religious instinct of the child can be related to a similar enlargement of the instinct of filial trust and dependence. The educator is therefore working within the two most fundamental childish qualities, qualities provoked and fostered by all right family life, with its relation of love to parents, brothers, sisters and friends; and may gently lead out these two mighty impulses to a fulfilment which, at maturity, embrace God and the whole world. The wise teacher, then, must work with the instincts, not against them: encouraging all kindly social feelings, all vigorous self-expression, wonder, trustfulness, love. Recognizing the paramount importance of emotion—for without emotional colour no idea can be actual to us, and no deed thoroughly and vigorously performed—yet he must always be on his guard against blocking the natural channels of human feeling, and giving them the opportunity of exploding under pious disguises in the religious sphere.

Here it is that the danger of too emotional a type of religious training comes in. Sentimentalism of all kinds is dangerous and objectionable, especially in the education of girls, whom it excites and debilitates. Boys are more often merely alienated by it. In both cases, the method of presentation which regards the spiritual life simply as a normal aspect of full human life is best. No artificial barrier should be set up between the sacred and the profane. The passion for truth and the passion for God should be treated as one: and that pursuit of knowledge for its own sake, those adventurous explorations of the mind, in which the more intelligent type of adolescent loves to try his growing powers, ought to be encouraged in the spiritual sphere as elsewhere. The results of research into religious origins should be explained without reservation, and no intellectual difficulty should be dodged. The putting-off method of meeting awkward questions, now generally recognized as dangerous in matters of natural history, is just as dangerous in the religious sphere. No teacher who is afraid to state his own position with perfect candour should ever be allowed to undertake this side of education; nor any in whom there is a marked cleavage between the standard of conduct and the standard of thought. The healthy adolescent is prompt to perceive inconsistency and unsparing in its condemnation.

Moreover, a most careful discrimination is daily becoming more necessary, in the teaching of traditional religion of a supernatural and non-empirical type. Many of its elements must no doubt be retained by us, for the child-mind demands firm outlines and examples and imagery drawn from the world of sense. Yet grave dangers are attached to it. On, the one hand an exclusive reliance on tradition paves the way for the disillusion which is so often experienced towards the end of adolescence, when it frequently causes a violent reaction to materialism. On the other hand it exposes us to a risk which we particularly want to avoid: that of reducing the child's nascent spiritual life to the dream level, to a fantasy in which it satisfies wishes that outward life leaves unfulfilled. Many pious people, especially those who tell us that their religion is a "comfort" to them, go through life in a spiritual day-dream of this kind. Concrete life has starved them of love, of beauty, of interest—it has given them no synthesis which satisfies the passionate human search for meaning—and they have found all this in a dream-world, made from the materials of conventional piety. If religion is thus allowed to become a ready-made day-dream it will certainly interest adolescents of a certain sort. The naturally introverted type will become meditative; whilst their opposites, the extroverted or active type, will probably tend to be ritualistic. But here again we are missing the essence of spiritual life.

Our aim should be to induce, in a wholesome way, that sense of the spiritual in daily experience which the old writers called the consciousness of the of God. The monastic training in spirituality, slowly evolved under pressure of experience, nearly always did this. It has bequeathed to us a funded wisdom of which we make little use; and this, reinterpreted in the light of psychological knowledge, might I believe cast a great deal of light on the fundamental problems of spiritual education. We could if we chose take many hints from it, as regards the disciplining of the attention, the correct use of suggestion, the teaching of meditation, the sublimation and direction to an assigned end of the natural impulse to reverie; above all, the education of the moral life. For character-building as understood by these old specialists was the most practical of arts.

Further, in all this teaching, those inward activities and responses to which we can give generally the name of prayer, and those outward activities and deeds of service to which we can give the name of work, ought to be trained together and never dissociated. They are the complementary and balanced expressions of one spirit of life: and must be given together, under appropriately simple forms. Concrete application of the child's energies, aptitudes and ideals must from the first run side by side with the teaching of principle. Young people therefore should constantly be encouraged to face as practical and interesting facts, not as formulæ, those reactions to eternal and this-world reality which used to be called our duty to God and our neighbour; and do concrete things proper to a real citizen of a really theocratic world. They must be made to realize that nothing is truly ours until we have expressed it in our deeds. Moreover, these deeds should not be easy. They should involve effort and self-sacrifice; and also some drudgery, which is worse. The spiritual life is only valued by those on whom it makes genuine demands. Almost any kind of service will do, which calls for attention, time and hard work. Though voluntary, it must not be casual: but, once undertaken, should be regarded as an honourable obligation. The Boy Scouts and Girl Guides have shown us how wide a choice of possible "good deeds" is offered by every community: and such a banding together of young people for corporate acts of service is strongly to be commended. It encourages unselfish comradeship, satisfies that "gang-instinct" which is a well-known character of adolescence, and should leave no opening for self-consciousness, rivalry, and vanity in well-doing or in abnegation.

Wise educators find that a combined system of organized games in which the social instinct can be expressed and developed, and of independent constructive work, in which the creative impulse can find satisfaction, best meets the corporate and creative needs of adolescence, favours the right development of character, and produces a harmonized life. On the level of the spiritual life too this principle is valid; and, guided by it, we should seek to give young people both corporate and personal work and experience. On the one hand, gregariousness is at its strongest in the healthy adolescent, the force of public opinion is more intensely felt than at any other time of life, that priceless quality the spirit of comradeship is most easily educed. We must therefore seek to give the spiritual life a vigorous corporate character; to make it "good form" for the school, and to use the team-spirit in the choir and the guild as well as in the cricket field. By an extension of this principle and under the influence of a suitable teacher, the school-mob may be transformed into a co-operative society animated by one joyous and unselfish spirit: all the great powers of social suggestion being freely used for the highest ends. Thus we may introduce the pupil, at his most plastic age, into a spiritual-social order and let him grow within it, developing those qualities and skills on which it makes demands. The religious exercises, whatever they are, should be in common, in order to develop the mass consciousness of the school and weld it into a real group. Music, songs, processions, etc., produce a feeling of unity, and encourage spiritual contagion. Services of an appropriate kind, if there be a chapel, or the opening of school with prayer and a hymn (which ought always to be followed by a short silence) provide a natural expression for corporate religious feeling: and remember that to give a feeling opportunity of voluntary expression is commonly to educe and affirm it. As regards active work, whilst school charities are an obvious field in which unselfish energies may be spent, many other openings will be found by enthusiastic teachers, and by the pupils whom their enthusiasm has inspired.

On the other hand, the spare-time occupations of the adolescent; the independent and self-chosen work, often most arduous and always absorbing, of making, planning, learning about things—and most of us can still remember how desperately important these seemed to us, whether our taste was for making engines, writing poetry, or collecting moths—these are of the greatest importance for his development. They give him something really his own, exercise his powers, train his attention, feed his creative instinct. They counteract those mechanical and conventional reactions to the world, which are induced by the merely traditional type of education, either of manners or of mind. And here, in the prudent encouragement of a personal interest in and dealing with the actual problems of conduct and even of belief—the most difficult of the educator's tasks—we guard against the merely acquiescent attitude of much adult piety, and foster from the beginning a vigorous personal interest, a first-hand contact with higher realities.

The heroic aspect of history may well form the second line in this attempt to capture education and use it in the interests of the spiritual life. By it we can best link up the actual and the ideal, and demonstrate the single character of human greatness; whether it be exhibited, in the physical or the supersensual sphere. Such a demonstration is most important; for so long as the spiritual life is regarded as merely a departmental thing, and its full development as a matter for specialists or saints, it will never produce its full effect in human affairs. We must exhibit it as the full flower of that Reality which inspires all human life. *"All* kinds of skill," said Tauler, "are gifts of the Holy Ghost," and he might have said, all kinds of beauty and all kinds of courage too.

The heroic makes a direct appeal to lads and girls, and is by far the safest way of approach to their emotions. The chivalrous, the noble, the

THE LIFE OF THE SPIRIT AND THE LIFE OF TO-DAY

desperately brave, attract the adolescent far more than passive goodness. That strong instinct of subjection, of homage, which he shows in his hero-worship, is a most valuable tool in the hands of the teacher who is seeking to lead him into greater fullness of life. Yet the range over which we seek material for his admiration is often deplorably narrow. We have behind us a great spiritual history, which shows the highest faculties of the soul in action: the power and the happiness they bring. Do we take enough notice of it? What about our English saints? I mean the real saints, not the official ones. Not St. George and St. Alban, about whom we know practically nothing: but, for instance, Lancelot Andrewes, John Wesley, Elizabeth Fry, about whom we know a great deal. Children, who find difficulty in general ideas, learn best from particular instances. Yet boys and girls who can give a coherent account of such stimulating personalities as Julius Caesar, William the Conqueror, Henry VIII. and his wives, or Napoleon—none of whom have so very much to tell us that bears on the permanent interests of the soul—do not as a rule possess any vivid idea, say, of Gautama, St. Benedict, Gregory the Great, St. Catherine of Siena, St. Francis Xavier, George Fox, St. Vincent de Paul and his friends: persons at least as significant, and far better worth meeting, than the military commanders and political adventurers of their time. The stories of the early Buddhists, the Sufi saints, St. Francis of Assisi, St. Ignatius, the early Quakers, the African missionaries, are full of things which can be made to interest even a young child. The legends which have grown up round some of them satisfy the instinct that draws it to fairy tales. They help it to dream well; and give to the developing mind food which it could assimilate in no other way. Older boys and girls, could they be given some idea of the spiritual heroes of Christendom as real men and women, without the nauseous note of piety which generally infects their biographies, would find much to delight them: romance of the best sort, because concerned with the highest values, and stories of endurance and courage such as always appeal to them. These people were not objectionable pietists. They were persons of fullest vitality and immense natural attraction; the pick of the race. We know that, by the numbers who left all to follow them. Ought we not to introduce our pupils to them; not as stuffed specimens, but as vivid human beings? Something might be done to create the right atmosphere for this, on the lines suggested by Dr. Hayward in that splendid little book "The Lesson in Appreciation." All that he says there about æsthetics, is applicable to any lesson dealing with the higher values of life. In this way, young people would be made to realize the spiritual life; not as something abnormal and more or less conventionalized, but as a golden thread running right through human history, and making demands on just those dynamic qualities which they feel themselves to possess. The adolescent is naturally vigorous and combative, and wants, above all else, something worth fighting for. This, too often, his teachers forget to provide.

The study of nature, and of æsthetics—including poetry—gives us yet another way of approach. The child should be introduced to these great worlds of life and of beauty, and encouraged but never forced to feed on the best they contain. By implication, but never by any method savouring of "uplift," these subjects should be related with that sense of the spiritual and of its immanence in creation, which ought to inspire the teacher; and with which it is his duty to infect his pupils if he can. Children may, very early, be taught or rather induced to look at natural things with that quietness, attention, and delight which are the beginnings of contemplation, and the conditions, under which nature reveals her real secrets to us. The child is a natural pagan, and often the first appeal to its nascent spiritual faculty is best made through its instinctive joy in the life of animals and flowers, the clouds and the winds. Here it may learn very easily that wonder and adoration, which are the gateways to the presence of God. In simple forms of verse, music, and rhythmical movement it can be encouraged—as the Salvation Army has discovered—to give this happy adoration a natural, dramatic, and rhythmic expression: for the young child, as we know, reproduces the mental condition of the primitive, and primitive forms of worship will suit it best.

It need hardly be said that education of the type we have been considering demands great gifts in the teacher: simplicity, enthusiasm, sympathy, and also a vigorous sense of humour, keeping him sharply aware of the narrow line that divides the priggish from the ideal. This education ought to inspire, but it ought not to replace, the fullest and most expert training of the body and mind; for the spirit needs a perfectly balanced machine, through which to express its life in the physical world. The actual additions to curriculum which it demands may be few: it is the attitude, the spirit, which must be changed. Specifically moral education, the building of character, will of course form an essential part of it: in fact must be present within it from the first. But this comes best without observation, and will be found to depend chiefly on the character of the teacher, the love, admiration and imitation he evokes, the ethical tone he gives. Childhood is of all ages the one most open to suggestion, and in this fact the educator finds at once his best opportunity and greatest responsibility.

Ruysbroeck has described to us the three outstanding moral dispositions in respect of God, of man, and of the conduct of life, which mark the true man or woman of the Spirit; and it is in the childhood that the tendency to these qualities must be acquired. First, he says,—I paraphrase, since the old terms of moral theology are no longer vivid to us—there comes an attitude of reverent love, of adoration, towards all that is holy, beautiful, or true. And next, from this, there grows up an attitude towards other men, governed by those qualities which are the essence of courtesy: patience, gentleness, kindness, and sympathy. These keep us both supple and generous in our responses to our social environment. Last, our creative energies are transfigured by an energetic love, an inward eagerness for every kind of work, which makes impossible all slackness and dullness of heart, and will impel us to live to the utmost the active life of service for which we are born.[4]

But these moral qualities cannot be taught; they are learned by imitation and infection, and developed by opportunity of action. The best agent of their propagation is an attractive personality in which they are dominant; for we know the universal tendency of young people to imitate those whom they admire. The relation between parent and child or master and pupil is therefore the central factor in any scheme of education which seeks to further the spiritual life. Only those who have already become real can communicate the knowledge of Reality. It is from the sportsman that we catch the spirit of fair-play, from the humble that we learn humility. The artist shows us beauty, the saint shows us God. It should therefore be the business of those in authority to search out and give scope to those who possess and are able to impart this triumphing spiritual life. A head-master who makes his boys live at their highest level and act on their noblest impulses, because he does it himself, is a person of supreme value to the State. It would be well if we cleared our minds of cant, and acknowledged that such a man alone is truly able to educate; since the spiritual life is infectious, but cannot be propagated by artificial means.

Finally, we have to remember that any attempt towards the education of the spirit—and such an attempt must surely be made by all who accept spiritual values as central for life—can only safely be undertaken with full knowledge of its special dangers and difficulties. These dangers and difficulties are connected with the instinctive and intellectual life of the child and the adolescent, who are growing, and growing unevenly, during the whole period of training. They are supple as regards other forces than those which we bring to bear on them; open to suggestion from many different levels of life.

Our greatest difficulty abides in the fact that, as we have seen, a vigorous spiritual life must give scope to the emotions. It is above all the heart rather than the mind which must be won for God. Yet, the greatest care must be exercised to ensure that the appeal to the emotions is free from all possibility of appeal to latent and uncomprehended natural instincts. This peril, to which current psychology gives perhaps too much attention, is nevertheless real. Candid students of religious history are bound to acknowledge the unfortunate part which it has often played in the past. These natural instincts fall into two great classes: those relating to self-preservation and those relating to the preservation of the race. The note of fear, the exaggerated longing for shelter and protection, the childish attitude of mere clinging dependence, fostered by religion of a certain type, are all oblique expressions of the instinct of self-preservation: and the rather feverish devotional moods and exuberant emotional expressions with which we are all familiar have, equally, a natural origin. Our task in the training of young people is to evoke enthusiasm, courage and love, without appealing to either of these sources of excitement. Generally speaking, it is safe to say that for this reason all sentimental and many anthropomorphic religious ideas are bad for lads and girls. These have, indeed, no part in that austere yet ardent love of God which inspires the real spiritual life.

Our aim ought to be, to teach and impress the reality of Spirit, its regnancy in human life, whilst the mind is alert and supple: and so to teach and impress it, that it is woven into the stuff of the mental and moral life and cannot seriously be injured by the hostile criticisms of the rationalist. Remember, that the prime object of education is the moulding of the unconscious and instinctive nature, the home of habit. If we can give this the desired tendency and tone of feeling, we can trust the rational mind to find good reasons with which to reinforce its attitudes and preferences. So it is not so much the specific belief, as the whole spiritual attitude to existence which we seek to affirm; and this will be done on the whole more effectively by the generalized suggestions which come to the pupil from his own surroundings, and the lives of those whom he admires, than by the limited and special suggestions of a creed. It is found that the less any desired motive is bound up with particular acts, persons, or ideas, the greater is the chance of its being universalized and made good for life all round. I do not intend by this statement to criticize any particular presentation of religion. Nevertheless, educators ought to remember that a religion which is first entirely bound up with narrow and childish theological ideas, and is then presented as true in the absolute sense, is bound to break down under greater knowledge or hostile criticism; and may then involve the disappearance of the religious impulse as a whole, at least for a long period.

Did we know our business, we ought surely to be able to ensure in our young people a steady and harmonious spiritual growth. The "conversion" or psychic convulsion which is sometimes regarded as an essential preliminary of any vivid awakening of the spiritual consciousness, is really a tribute exacted by our wrong educational methods. It is a proof that we have allowed the plastic creature confided to us to harden in the wrong shape. But if, side by side and in simplest language, we teach the conceptions: first, of God as the transcendent yet indwelling Spirit of love, of beauty and of power; next, of man's constant dependence on Him and possible contact with His nature in that arduous and loving act of attention which is the essence of prayer; last, of unselfish work and fellowship as the necessary expressions of all human ideals—then, I think, we may hope to lay the foundations of a balanced and a wholesome life, in which man's various faculties work together for good, and his vigorous instinctive life is directed to the highest ends.

---

1. Spencer: "Education," Cap. 1.
2. Jones and Muirhead: "Life and Philosophy of Edward Caird," pp. 64, 65.
3. "The Cloud of Unknowing," Cap. 39.
4. Ruysbroeck: "The Adornment of the Spiritual Marriage," Bk. I, Caps. 12-24.

CHAPTER VIII

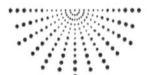

THE LIFE OF THE SPIRIT AND THE SOCIAL ORDER

We have come to the last chapter of this book; and I am conscious that those who have had the patience to follow its argument from the beginning, may now feel a certain sense of incompleteness. They will observe that, though many things have been said about the life of the Spirit, not a great deal seems to have been said, at any rate directly, about the second half of the title—the life of to-day—and especially about those very important aspects of our modern active life which are resumed in the word Social. This avoidance has been, at least in part, intentional. We have witnessed in this century a violent revulsion from the individualistic type of religion; a revulsion which parallels upon its own levels, and indeed is a part of, the revolt from Victorian individualism in political economic life. Those who come much into contact with students, and with the younger and more vigorous clergy, are aware how far this revolt has proceeded: how completely, in the minds of those young people who are interested in religion, the Social Gospel now overpowers all other aspects of the spiritual life. Again and again we are assured by the most earnest among them that in their view religion is a social activity, and service is its proper expression: that all valid knowledge of God is social, and He is chiefly known in mankind: that the use of prayer is mainly social, in that it improves us for service, otherwise it must be condemned as a merely selfish activity: finally, that the true meaning and value of suffering are social too. A visitor to a recent Swanwick Conference of the Student Christian Movement has publicly expressed his regret that some students still seemed to be concerned with the problems of their own spiritual life; and were not prepared to let that look after itself, whilst they started straight off to work for the social realization of the Kingdom of God. When a great truth becomes exaggerated to this extent, and is held to the exclusion of its compensating opposite, it is in a fair way to becoming a lie. And we have here, I think, a real confusion of ideas which will, if allowed to continue, react unfavourably upon the religion of the future; because it gives away the most sacred conviction of the idealist, the belief in the absolute character of spiritual values, and in the effort to win them as the great activity of man. Social service, since it is one form of such an effort, a bringing in of more order, beauty, joy, is a fundamental duty—the fundamental duty—of the active life. Man does not truly love the Perfect until he is driven thus to seek its incarnation in the world of time. No one doubts this. All spiritual teachers have said it, in one way or another, for centuries. The mere fact that they feel impelled to teach at all, instead of saying "My secret to myself"—which is so much easier and pleasanter to the natural contemplative—is a guarantee of the claim to service which they feel that love lays upon them. But this does not make such service of man, however devoted, either the same thing as the search for, response to, intercourse with God; or, a sufficient substitute for these specifically spiritual acts.

Plainly, we are called upon to strive with all our power to bring in the Kingdom; that is, to incarnate in the time world the highest spiritual values which we have known. But our ability to do this is strictly dependent on those values being known, at least by some of us, at first-hand; and for this first-hand perception, as we have seen, the soul must have a measure of solitude and silence. Therefore, if the swing-over to a purely social interpretation of religion be allowed to continue unchecked, the result can only be an impoverishment of our spiritual life; quite as far-reaching and as regrettable as that which follows from an unbridled individualism. Without the inner life of prayer and-meditation, lived for its own sake and for no utilitarian motive, neither our judgments upon the social order nor our active social service will be perfectly performed; because they will not be the channel of Creative Spirit expressing itself through us in the world of to-day.

Christ, it is true, gives nobody any encouragement for supposing that a merely self-cultivating sort of spirituality, keeping the home fires burning and so on, is anybody's main job. The main job confided to His friends is the preaching of the Gospel. That is, spreading Reality, teaching it, inserting it into existence; by prayers, words, acts, and also if need be by manual work, and always under the conditions and symbolisms of our contemporary world. But since we can only give others that which we already possess, this presupposes that we have got something of Reality as a living, burning fire in ourselves. The soul's two activities of reception and donation must be held in balance, or impotence and unreality will result. It is only out of the heart of his own experience that man really helps his neighbour: and thus there is an ultimate social value in the most secret responses of the soul to grace. No one, for instance, can help others to repentance who has not known it at first-hand. Therefore we have to keep the home fires burning, because they are the fires which raise the steam that does the work: and we do this mostly by the fuel with which we feed them, though partly too by giving free access to currents of fresh air from the outer world.

We cannot read St. Paul's letters with sympathy and escape the conviction that in the midst of his great missionary efforts he was profoundly concerned too with the problems of his own inner life. The little bits of self-revelation that break into the epistles and, threaded together, show us the curve of his growth, also show us how much, lay behind them, how intense, and how exacting was the inward travail that accompanied his outward deeds. Here he is representative of the true apostolic type. It is because St. Augustine is the man of the "Confessions" that he is also the creator of "The City of God." The regenerative work of St. Francis was accompanied by an unremitting life of penitence and recollection. Fox and Wesley, abounding in labours, yet never relaxed the tension of their soul's effort to correspond with a transcendent Reality. These and many other examples warn us that only by such a sustained and double movement can the man of the Spirit actualize all his possibilities and do his real work. He must, says Ruysbroeck, "both ascend and descend with love."[1] On any other basis he misses the richness of that fully integrated human existence "swinging between the unseen and the seen" in which the social and individual, incorporated and solitary responses to the demands of Spirit are fully carried through. Instead, he exhibits restriction and lack balance. This in the end must react as unfavourably on the social as on the personal side of life: since the place and influence of the spiritual life in the social order will depend entirely on its place in the individual consciousness of which that social order will be built, the extent in which loyalty to the one Spirit governs their reactions to common daily experience.

Here then, as in so much else, the ideal is not an arbitrary choice but a struck balance. First, a personal contact with Eternal Reality, deepening, illuminating and enlarging all of our experience of fact, all our responses to it: that is, faith. Next, the fullest possible sense of our membership of and duty towards the social organism, a completely rich, various, heroic, self-giving, social life: that is, charity. The dissociation of these two sides of human experience is fatal to that divine hope which should crown and unite them; and which represents the human instinct for novelty in a sublimated form.

It is of course true that social groups may be regenerated. The success of such group-formations as the primitive Franciscans, the Friends of God, the Quakers, the Salvation Army, demonstrates this. But groups, in the last resort, consist of individuals, who must each be regenerated one by one; whose outlook, if they are to be whole men, must include in its span abiding values as well as the stream of time, and who, for the full development of this their two-fold destiny, require each a measure both of solitude and of association. Hence it follows, that the final answer to the repeated question: "Does God save men, does Spirit work towards the regeneration of humanity (the same thing), one by one, or in groups?" is this: that the proposed alternative is illusory. We cannot say that the Divine action in the world as we know it, is either merely social or merely individual; but both. And the next question—a highly practical question—is, "How *both*?" For the answer to this, if we can find it, will give us at last a formula by which we can true up our own effort toward completeness of self-expression in the here-and-now.

How, then, are groups of men moved up to higher spiritual levels; helped to such an actual possession of power and love and a sound mind as shall transfigure and perfect their lives? For this, more than all else, is what we now want to achieve. I speak in generalities, and of average human nature, not of these specially sensitive or gifted individuals who are themselves the revealers of Reality to their fellow-men.

History suggests, I think, that this group-regeneration is effected in the last resort through a special sublimation of the herd-instinct; that is, the full and willing use on spiritual levels of the characters which are inherent in human gregariousness.[2] We have looked at some of these characters in past chapters. Our study of them suggests, that the first stage in any social regeneration is likely to be brought about by the instinctive rallying of individuals about a natural leader, strong enough to compel and direct them; and whose appeal is to the impulsive life, to an acknowledged of unacknowledged lack or craving, not to the faculty of deliberate choice. This leader, then, must offer new life and love, not intellectual solutions. He must be able to share with his flock his own ardour and apprehension of Reality; and evoke from them the profound human impulse to imitation. They will catch his enthusiasm, and thus receive the suggestions of his teaching and of his life. This first stage, supremely illustrated in the disciples of Christ, and again in the groups who gathered round such men as St. Francis, Fox, or Booth, is re-experienced in a lesser way in every successful revival: and each genuine restoration of the life of Spirit, whether its declared aim be social or religious, has a certain revivalistic character. We must therefore keep an eye on these principles of discipleship and contagion, as likely to govern any future spiritualization of our own social life; looking for the beginnings of true reconstruction, not to the general dissemination of suitable doctrines, but to the living burning influence of an ardent soul. And I may add here, as the corollary of this conclusion, first that the evoking and fostering of such ardour is in itself a piece of social service of the highest value, and next that it makes every individual socially responsible for the due sharing of even the small measure of ardour, certitude or power he or she has received. We are to be conductors of the Divine energy; not to insulate it. There is of course nothing new in all this: but there is nothing new fundamentally in the spiritual life, save in St. Augustine's sense of the eternal youth and freshness of all beauty.[3] The only novelty which we can safely introduce will be in the terms in which we describe it; the perpetual new exhibition of it within the time-world, the fresh and various applications which we can give to its abiding laws, in the special circumstances and opportunities of our own day.

But the influence of the crowd-compeller, the leader, whether in the crude form of the revivalist or in the more penetrating and enduring form of the creative mystic or religious founder, the loyalty and imitation of the disciple, the corporate and generalized enthusiasm of the group can only be the first educative phase in any veritable incarnation of Spirit upon earth. Each member of the herd is now committed to the fullest personal living-out of the new life he has received. Only in so far as the first stage of suggestion and imitation is carried over to the next stage of personal actualization, can we say that there is any real promotion of spiritual *life*: any hope that this life will work a true renovation of the group into which it has been inserted and achieve the social phase.

If, then, it does achieve the social phase what stages may we expect it to pass through, and by what special characters will it be graced?

Let us look back for a moment at some of our conclusions about the individual life. We said that this life, if fully lived, exhibited the four characters of work and contemplation, self-discipline and service: deepening and incarnating within its own various this-world experience its other-world apprehensions of Eternity, of God. Its temper should thus be both social and ascetic. It should be doubly based, on humility and on given power. Now the social order—more exactly, the social organism—in which Spirit is really to triumph, can only be built up of individuals who do with a greater or less perfection and intensity exhibit these characters, some upon independent levels of creative freedom, some on those of discipleship: for here all men are not equal, and it is humbug to pretend that they are. This social order, being so built of regenerate units, would be dominated by these same implicits of the regenerate consciousness; and would tend to solve in their light the special problems of community life. And this unity of aim would really make of it one body; the body of a fully socialized *and* fully spiritualized humanity, which perhaps we might without presumption describe as indeed the son of God.

The life of such a social organism, its growth, its cycle of corporate behaviour, would be strung on that same fourfold cord which combined the desires and deeds of the regenerate self into a series: namely, Penitence, Surrender, Recollection, and Work. It would be actuated first by a real social repentance. That is, by a turning from that constant capitulation to its past, to animal and savage impulse, the power of which our generation at least knows only too well; and by the complementary effort to unify vigorous instinctive action and social conscience. I think every one can find for themselves some sphere, national, racial, industrial, financial, in which social penitence could work; and the constant corporate fall-back into sin, which we now disguise as human nature, or sometimes—even more insincerely—as economic and political necessity, might be faced and called by its true name. Such a social penitence—such a corporate realization of the mess that we have made of things—is as much a direct movement of the Spirit, and as great an essential of regeneration, as any individual movement of the broken and contrite heart.

Could a quick social conscience, aware of obligations to Reality which do not end with making this world a comfortable place—though we have not even managed that for the majority of men—feel quite at ease, say, after an unflinching survey of our present system of State punishment? Or after reading the unvarnished record of our dealings with the problem of Indian immigration into Africa? Or after considering the inner nature of international diplomacy and finance? Or even, to come nearer home, after a stroll through Hoxton: the sort of place, it is true, which we have not exactly made on purpose but which has made itself because we have not, as a community, exercised our undoubted powers of choice and action in an intelligent and loving way. Can we justify the peculiar characteristics of Hoxton: congratulate ourselves on the amount of light, air and beauty which its inhabitants enjoy, the sort of children that are reared in it, as the best we can do towards furthering the racial aim? It is a monument of stupidity no less than of meanness. Yet the conception of God which the whole religious experience of growing man presses on us, suggests that both intelligence and love ought to characterize His ideal for human life. Look then at these, and all the other things of the same kind. Look at our attitude towards prostitution, at the drink traffic, at the ugliness and injustice of the many institutions which we allow to endure. Look at them in the Universal Spirit; and then consider, whether a searching corporate repentance is not really the inevitable preliminary of a social and spiritual advance. All these things have happened because we have as a body consistently fallen below our best possible, lacked courage to incarnate our vision in the political sphere. Instead, we have, acted on the crowd level, swayed by unsublimated instincts of acquisition, disguised lust, self-preservation, self-assertion, and ignoble fear: and such a fall-back is the very essence of social sin.

We have made many plans and elevations; but we have not really tried to build Jerusalem either in our own hearts or in "England's pleasant land." Blake thought that the preliminary of such a building up of the harmonious social order must be the building up or harmonizing of men, of each man; and when this essential work was really done, Heaven's "Countenance Divine" would suddenly declare itself "among the dark Satanic mills."[4] What was wrong with man, and ultimately therefore with society, was the cleavage between his "Spectre" or energetic intelligence, and "Emanation" or loving imagination. Divided, they only tormented one another. United, they were the material of divine humanity. Now the complementary affirmative movement which shall balance and complete true social penitence will be just such a unification and dedication of society's best energies and noblest ideals, now commonly separated. The Spectre is attending to economics: the Emanation is dreaming of Utopia. We want to see them united, for from this union alone will come the social aspect for surrender. That is to say, a single-minded, unselfish yielding to those good social impulses which we all feel from time to time, and might take more seriously did, we realize them as the impulsions of holy and creative Spirit pressing us towards novelty, giving us our chance; our small actualization of the universal tendency to the Divine. As it is, we do feel a little uncomfortable when these stirrings reach us; but commonly console ourselves with the thought that their realization is at present outside the sphere of practical politics. Yet the obligation of response to those stirrings is laid on all who feel them; and unless some will first make this venture of faith, our possible future will never be achieved. Christ was born among those who *expected* the Kingdom of God. The favouring atmosphere of His childhood is suggested by these words. It is our business to prepare, so far as we may, a favourable atmosphere and environment for the children who will make the future: and this environment is not anything mysterious, it is simply ourselves. The men and women who are now coming to maturity, still supple to experience and capable of enthusiastic and disinterested choice—that is, of surrender in the noblest sense—will have great opportunities of influencing those who are younger than themselves. The torch is being offered to them; and it is of vital importance to the unborn future that they should grasp and hand it on, without worrying about whether their fingers are going to be burnt. If they do grasp it, they may prove to be the bringers in of a new world, a fresh and vigorous social order, which is based upon true values, controlled by a spiritual conception of life; a world in which this factor is as freely acknowledged by all normal persons, as is the movement of the earth round the sun.

I do not speak here of fantastic dreams about Utopias, or of the coloured pictures of the apocalyptic imagination; but of a concrete genuine possibility, at which clear-sighted persons have hinted again and again. Consider our racial past. Look at the Piltdown skull: reconstruct the person or creature whose brain that skull contained, and actualize the directions in which his imperious instincts, his vaguely conscious will and desire, were pressing into life. They too were expressions of Creative Spirit; and there is perfect continuity between his vital impulse and our own. Now, consider one of the better achievements of civilization; say the life of a University, with its devotion to disinterested learning, its conservation of old beauty and quest of new truth. Even if we take its lowest common measure, the transfiguration of desire is considerable. Yet in the things of the Spirit we must surely acknowledge ourselves still to be primitive men; and no one can say that it yet appears what we shall be. All really depends on the direction in which human society decides to push into experience, the surrender which it makes to the impulsion of the Spirit; how its tendency to novelty is employed, the sort of complex habits which are formed by it, as more and more crude social instinct is lifted up into conscious intention, and given the precision of thought.

In our regenerate society, then, if we ever get it, the balanced moods of Repentance of our racial past and Surrender to our spiritual calling, the pull-forward of the Spirit of Life even in its most austere difficult demands, will control us; as being the socialized extensions of these same attitudes of the individual soul. And they will press the community to those same balanced expressions of its instinct for reality, which completed the individual life: that is to say, to Recollection and Work. In the furnishing of a frame for the regular social exercise of recollection—the gathering in of the corporate mind and its direction to eternal values, the abiding foundations of existence; the consideration of all its problems in silence and peace; the dramatic and sacramental expression of its unity and of its dependence on the higher powers of life—in all this, the institutional religion of the future will perhaps find its true sphere of action, and take its rightful place in the socialized life of the Spirit.

Finally, the work which is done by a community of which the inner life is controlled by these three factors will be the concrete expression of these factors in the time-world; and will perpetuate and hand on all that is noble, stable and reasonable in human discovery and tradition, whether in the sphere of conduct, of thought, of creation, of manual labour, or the control of nature, whilst remaining supple towards the demands and gifts of novelty. New value will be given to craftsmanship and a sense of dedication—now almost unknown—to those who direct it. Consider the effect of this attitude on worker, trader, designer, employer: how many questions would then answer themselves, how many sore places would be healed.

It is not necessary, in order to take sides with this possible new order and work for it, that we should commit ourselves to any one party or scheme of social reform. Still less is it necessary to suppose such reform the only field in which the active and social side of the spiritual life is to be lived. Repentance, surrender, recollection and industry can do their transfiguring work in art, science, craftsmanship, scholarship, and play: making all these things more representative of reality, nearer our own best possible, and so more vivid and worth while. If Tauler was right, and all kinds of skill are gifts of the Holy Ghost—a proposition which no thorough-going theist can refuse—then will not a reference back on the part of the worker to that fontal source of power make for humility and perfection in all work? Personally I am not at all afraid to recognize a spiritual element in all good craftsmanship, in the delighted and diligent creation of the fine potter, smith or carpenter, in the well-tended garden and beehive, the perfectly adjusted home; for do not all these help the explication of the one Spirit of Life in the diversity of His gifts?

The full life of the Spirit must be more rich and various in its expression than any life that we have yet known, and find place for every worthy and delightful activity. It does not in the least mean a bloodless goodness; a refusal of fun and everlasting fuss about uplift. But it does mean looking at and judging each problem in a particular light, and acting on that judgment without fear. Were this principle established, and society poised on this centre, reforms would follow its application almost automatically; specific evils would retreat. New knowledge of beauty would reveal the ugliness of many satisfactions which we now offer to ourselves, and new love the defective character of many of our social relations. Certain things would therefore leave off happening, would go; because the direction of desire had changed. I do not wish to particularize, for this only means blurring the issue by putting forward one's own pet reforms. But I cannot help pointing out that we shall never get spiritual values out of a society harried and tormented by economic pressure, or men and women whose whole attention is given up to the daily task of keeping alive. This is not a political statement: it is a plain fact that we must face. Though the courageous lives of the poor, their patient endurance of insecurity may reveal a nobility that shames us, it still remains true that these lives do not represent the most favourable conditions of the soul. It is not poverty that matters; but strain and the presence of anxiety and fear, the impossibility of detachment. Therefore this oppression at least would have to be lightened, before the social conscience could be at ease. Moreover as society advances along this way, every—even the most subtle—kind of cruelty and exploitation of self-advantage obtained to the detriment of other individuals, must tend to be eliminated; because here the drag-back of the past will be more and more completely conquered, its instincts fully sublimated, and no one will care to do those things any more. Bringing new feelings and more real concepts to our contact with our environment, we shall, in accordance with the law of apperception, see this environment in a different way; and so obtain from it a fresh series of experiences. The scale of pain and pleasure will be altered. We shall feel a searching responsibility about the way in which our money is made, and about any disadvantages to others which our amusements or comforts may involve.

Here, perhaps, it is well to register a protest against the curious but prevalent notion that any such concentrated effort for the spiritualization of society must tend to work itself out in the direction of a maudlin humanitarianism, a soft and sentimental reading of life. This idea merely advertises once more the fact that we still have a very mean and imperfect conception of God, and have made the mistake of setting up a water-tight bulkhead; between His revelation, in nature and His discovery in the life of prayer. It shows a failure to appreciate the stern, heroic aspect of Reality; the element of austerity in all genuine religion, the distinction between love and sentimentalism, the rightful place of risk, effort, even suffering, in all full achievement and all joy. If we are surrendered in love to the purposes of the Spirit, we are committed to the bringing out of the best possible in life; and this is a hard business, involving a quite definite social struggle with evil and atavism, in which some one is likely to be hurt. But surely that manly spirit of adventure which has driven men to the North Pole and the desert, and made them battle with delight against apparently impossible odds, can here find its appropriate sublimation?

If anyone who has followed these arguments, and now desires to bring them from idea into practice, asks: "What next?" the answer simply is— Begin. Begin with ourselves; and if possible, do not begin in solitude. "The basal principles of all collective life," says McDougall, "are sympathetic contagion, mass suggestion, imitation":[5] and again and again the history of spiritual experience illustrates this law, that its propagation is most often by way of discipleship and the corporate life, not by the intensive culture of purely solitary effort. It is for those who believe in the spiritual life to take full advantage now of this social suggestibility of man; though without any detraction from the prime importance of the personal spiritual life. Therefore, join up with somebody, find fellowship; whether it be in a church or society, or among a few like-minded friends. Draw together for mutual support, and face those imperatives of prayer and work which we have seen to be the condition of the fullest living-out of our existence. Fix and keep a reasonably balanced daily rule. Accept leadership where you find it—give it, if you feel the impulse and the strength. Do not wait for some grand opportunity, and whilst you are waiting stiffen in the wrong shape. The great opportunity may not be for us, but for the generation whose path we now prepare: and we do our best towards such preparation, if we begin in a small and humble way the incorporation of our hopes and desires as for instance Wesley and the Oxford Methodists did. They sought merely to put their own deeply felt ideas into action quite simply and without fuss; and we know how far the resulting impulse spread. The Bab movement in the East, the Salvation Army at home, show us this principle still operative; what a "little flock" dominated by a suitable herd-leader and swayed by love and adoration can do—and these, like Christianity itself, began as small and inconspicuous groups. It may be that our hope for the future depends on the formation of such groups—hives of the Spirit—in which the worker of every grade, the thinker, the artist, might each have their place: obtaining from incorporation the herd-advantages of mutual protection and unity of aim, and forming nuclei to which others could adhere.

Such a small group—and I am now thinking of something quite practical, say to begin with a study-circle, or a company of like-minded friends with a definite rule of life—may not seem to the outward eye very impressive. Regarded as a unit, it will even tend to be inferior to its best members: but it will be superior to the weakest, and with its leader will possess a dynamic character and reproductive power which he could never have exhibited alone. It should form a compact organization, both fervent and business-like; and might take as its ideal a combination of the characteristic temper of the contemplative order, with that of active and intelligent Christianity as seen in the best type of social settlement. This double character of inwardness and practicality seems to me to be essential to its success; and incorporation will certainly help it to be maintained. The rule should be simple and unostentatious, and need indeed be little more than the "heavenly rule" of faith, hope, and charity. This will involve first the realization of man's true life within a spiritual world-order, his utter dependence upon its realities and powers of communion with them; next his infinite possibilities of recovery and advancement; last his duty of love to all other selves and things. This triple law would be applied without shirking to every problem of existence; and the corporate spirit would be encouraged by meetings, by associated prayer, and specially I hope by the practice of corporate silence. Such a group would never permit the intrusion of the controversial element, but would be based on mutual trust; and the fact that all the members shared substantially the same view of human life, strove though in differing ways for the same ideals, were filled by the same enthusiasms, would allow the problems and experiences of the Spirit to be accepted as real, and discussed with frankness and simplicity. Thus oases of prayer and clear thinking might be created in our social wilderness, gradually developing such power and group-consciousness as we see in really living religious bodies. The group would probably make some definite piece of social work, or some definite question, specially its own. Seeking to judge the problem this presented in the Universal Spirit, it would work towards a solution, using for this purpose both heart and head. It would strive in regard to the special province chosen and solution reached to make its weight felt, either locally or nationally, in a way the individual could never hope to do; and might reasonably hope that its conclusions and its actions would exceed in balance and sanity those which any one of the members could have achieved alone.

I think that these groups would develop their own discipline, not borrow its details from the past: for they would soon find that some drill was necessary to them, and that luxury, idleness, self-indulgence and indifference to the common-good were in conflict with the inner spirit of the herd. They would inevitably come to practise that sane asceticism, not incompatible with gaiety of heart, which consists in concentration on the real, and quiet avoidance of the attractive sham. Plainness and simplicity do help the spiritual life, and these are more easy and wholesome when practised in common than when they are displayed by individuals in defiance of the social order that surrounds them. The differences of temperament and of spiritual level in the group members would prevent monotony; and insure that variety of reaction to the life of the Spirit which we so much wish to preserve. Those whose chief gift was for action would thus be directly supported by those natural contemplatives who might, if they remained in solitude, find it difficult to make their special gift serve their fellows as it must. Group-consciousness would cause the spreading and equalization of that spiritual sensitiveness which is, as a matter of fact, very unequally distributed amongst men. And in the backing up of the predominantly active workers by the organized prayerful will of the group, all the real values of intercession would be obtained: for this has really nothing to do with trying to persuade God to do specific acts, it is a particular way of exerting love, and thus of reaching and using spiritual power.

This incorporation, as I see it, would be made for the express purpose of getting driving force with which to act directly upon life. For spirituality, as we have seen all along, must not be a lovely fluid notion or a merely self-regarding education; but an education for action, for the insertion of eternal values into the time-world, in conformity with the incarnational philosophy which justifies it. Such action—such Insertion—depends on constant recourse to the sources of spiritual power. At present we tend to starve our possible centres of regeneration, or let them starve themselves, by our encouragement of the active at the expense of the contemplative life; and till this is mended, we shall get nothing really done. Forgetting St. Teresa's warning, that to give our Lord a perfect service, Martha and Mary must combine,[6] we represent the service of man as being itself an attention to God; and thus drain our best workers of their energies, and leave them no leisure for taking in Fresh supplies. Often they are wearied and confused by the multiplicity in which they must struggle; and they are not taught and encouraged to seek the healing experience of unity. Hence even our noblest teachers often show painful signs of spiritual exhaustion, and tend to relapse into the formal repetition of a message which was once a burning fire.

The continued force of any regenerative movement depends above all else on continued vivid contact with the Divine order, for the problems of the reformer are only really understood and seen in true proportion in its light. Such contact is not always easy: it is a form of work. After a time the weary and discouraged will need the support of discipline if they are to do it. Therefore definite role of silence and withdrawal—perhaps an extension of that system of periodical retreats which is one of the most hopeful features of contemporary religious life—is essential to any group-scheme for the general and social furtherance of the spiritual life. It is not to be denied for a moment, that countless good men and women who love the world in the divine and not in the self-regarding sense, are busy all their lives long in forwarding the purposes of the Spirit: which is acting through them, as truly as through the conscious prophets and regenerators of the race. But, to return for a moment to psychological language, whilst the Divine impulsion remains for us below the threshold, it is not doing all that it could for us nor we all that we could do for it; for we are not completely unified. We can by appropriate education bring up that imperative yet dim impulsion to conscious realization, and wittingly dedicate to its uses our heart, mind and will; and such realization in its most perfect form appears to be the psychological equivalent of the state which is described by spiritual writers, in their own special language, as "union with God."

I have been at some pains to avoid the use of this special language of the mystics; but now perhaps we may remind ourselves that, by the declaration of all who have achieved it, the mature spiritual life is such a condition of completed harmony—such a theopathetic state. Therefore here today, in the worst confusions of our social scramble, no less that in the

Indian forest or the mediæval cloister, man's really religious method and self-expression must be harmonious with a life-process of which this is the recognized if distant goal: and in all the work of restatement, this abiding objective must be kept in view. Such union, such full identification with the Divine purpose, must be a social as well as an individual expression of full life. It cannot be satisfied by the mere picking out of crumbs of perfection from the welter, but must mean in the end that the real interests of society are indentical with the interests of Creative Spirit, in so far as these are felt and known by man; the interests, that is, of a love that is energy and an energy that is love. Towards this identification, the willed tendency of each truly awakened individual must steadfastly be set; and also the corporate desire of each group, as expressed in its prayer and work. For the whole secret of life lies in directed desire.

A wide-spreading love to all in common, says Ruysbroeck in a celebrated passage, is the authentic mark of a truly spiritual man.[7] In this phrase is concealed the link between the social and personal aspects of the spiritual life. It means that our passional nature with its cravings and ardours, instead of making self-centred whirlpools, flows out in streams of charity and power towards all life. And we observe too that the Ninth Perfection of the Buddhist is such a state of active charity. "In his loving, sympathizing, joyful and steadfast mind he will recognize himself in all things, and will shed warmth and light on the world in all directions out of his great, deep, unbounded heart."[8]

Let this, then, be the teleological objective on which the will and the desire of individual and group are set: and let us ask what it involves, and how it is achieved. It involves all the ardour, tenderness and idealism of the lover, spent not on one chosen object but on all living things. Thus it means an immense widening of the arc of human sympathy; and this it is not possible to do properly, unless we have found the centre of the circle first. The glaring defect of current religion—I mean the vigorous kind, not the kind that is responsible for empty churches—is that it spends so much time in running round the arc, and rather takes the centre for granted. We see a great deal of love in generous-minded people, but also a good many gaps in it which reference to the centre might help us to find and to mend. Some Christian people seem to have a difficulty about loving reactionaries, and some about loving revolutionaries. And in institutional religion there are people of real ardour, called by those beautiful names Catholic and Evangelical, who do not seem able to see each other in the light of this wide-spreading love. Yet they would meet at the centre. And it is at the centre that the real life of the Spirit aims first; thence flowing out to the circumference—even to its most harsh, dark, difficult and rugged limits—in unbroken streams of generous love.

Such love is creative. It does not flow along the easy paths, spending itself on the attractive. It cuts new channels, goes where it is needed, and has as its special vocation—a vocation identical with that of the great artist—the "loving of the unlovely into lovableness." Thus does it participate according to its measure in the work of Divine incarnation. This does not mean a maudlin optimism, or any other kind of sentimentality; for as we delve more deeply into life, we always leave sentimentality behind. But it does mean a love which is based on a deep understanding of man's slow struggles and of the unequal movements of life, and is expressed in both arduous and highly skillful actions. It means taking the grimy, degraded, misshapen, and trying to get them right; because we feel that essentially they can be right. And further, of course, it means getting behind them to the conditions that control their wrongness; and getting these right if we can. Consider what human society would be if each of its members—not merely occasional philanthropists, idealists or saints, but financiers, politicians, traders, employers, employed—had this quality of spreading a creative love: if the whole impulse of life in every man and woman were towards such a harmony, first with God, and then with all other things and souls. There is nothing unnatural in this conception. It only means that our vital energy would flow in its real channel at last. Where then would be our most heart-searching social problems? The social order then would really be an order; tallying with St. Augustine's definition of a virtuous life as the ordering of love.

What about the master and the worker in such a possibly regenerated social order? Consider alone the immense release of energy for work needing to be done, if the civil wars of civilized man could cease and be replaced by that other mental fight, for the upbuilding of Jerusalem: how the impulse of Creative Spirit, surely working in humanity, would find the way made clear. Would not this, at last, actualize the Pauline dream, of each single citizen as a member of the Body of Christ? It is because we are not thus attuned to life, and surrendered to it, that our social confusion arises; the conflict of impulse within society simply mirrors the conflict of impulse within each individual mind.

We know that some of the greatest movements of history, veritable transformations of the group-mind, can be traced back to a tiny beginning in the faithful spiritual experience and response of some one man, his contact with the centre which started the ripples of creative love. If, then, we could elevate such universalized individuals into the position of herd-leaders, spread their secret, persuade society first to imitate them, and then to share their point of view, the real and sane, because love-impelled social revolution might begin. It will begin, when more and ever more people find themselves unable to participate in, or reap advantage from, the things which conflict with love: when tender emotion in man is so universalized, that it controls the instincts of acquisitiveness and of self-assertion. There are already for each of us some things in which we cannot participate, because they conflict too flagrantly with some aspect of our love, either for truth, or for justice, or for humanity, or for God; and these things each individual, according to his own level of realization, is bound to oppose without compromise. Most of us have enough widespreading love to be—for instance—quite free from temptation to be cruel, at any rate directly, to children or to animals. I say nothing about the indirect tortures which our sloth and insensitiveness still permit. Were these first flickers made ardent, and did they control all our reactions to life—and there is nothing abnormal, no break in continuity involved in this, only a reasonable growth—then, new paths of social discharge would have been made for our chief desires and impulses; and along these they would tend more and more to flow freely and easily, establishing new social-habits, unhampered by solicitations from our savage past. To us already, on the whole, these solicitations are less insistent than they were to the men of earlier centuries. We see their gradual defeat in slave emancipation, factory acts, increased religious tolerance, every movement towards social justice, every increase of the arc over which our obligations to other men obtain. They must now disguise themselves as patriotic or economic necessities, if we are to listen to them: as, in the Freudian dream, our hidden unworthy wishes slip through into consciousness in a symbolic form. But when their energy has been fully sublimated, the social action will no longer be a conflict but a harmony. Then we shall live the life of Spirit; and from this life will flow all love-inspired reform.

Yet we are, above all, to avoid the conclusion that the spiritual life, in its social expression, shall necessarily push us towards mere change; that novelty contains everything, and stability nothing, of the will of the Spirit for the race. Surely our aim shall be this: that religious sensitiveness shall spread, as our discovery of religion in the universe spreads, so that at last every man's reaction to the whole of experience shall be entinctured with Reality, coloured by this dominant feeling-tone. Spirit would then work

THE LIFE OF THE SPIRIT AND THE LIFE OF TO-DAY

from within outwards, and all life personal and social, mental and physical, would be moulded by its inspiring power. And in looking here for our best hope of development, we remain safely within history; and do not strive for any desperate pulling down or false simplification of our complex existence, such as has wrecked many attempts to spiritualize society in the past.

Consider the way by which we have come. We found in man an instinct for a spiritual Reality. A single, concrete, objective Fact, transcending yet informing his universe, compels his adoration, and is apperceived by him in three main ways. First, as the very Being, Heart and Meaning of that universe, the universal of all universals, next as a Presence including and exceeding the best that personality can mean to him, last as an indwelling and energizing Life. We saw in history the persistent emergence of a human type so fully aware of this Reality as to subdue to its interests all the activities of life; ever seeking to incarnate its abiding values in the world of time. And further, psychology suggested to us, even in its tentative new findings, its exploration of our strange mental deeps, reason for holding such surrender to the purposes of the Spirit to represent the condition of man's fullest psychic health, and access to his real sources of power. We found in the universal existence of religious institutions further evidence of this profound human need of spirituality. We saw there the often sharp and sky-piercing intensity of the individual aptitude for Reality enveloped, tempered and made wholesome by the social influences of the cultus and the group: made too, available for the community by the symbolisms that cultus had preserved. So that gradually the life of the Spirit emerged for us as something most actual, not archaic: a perennial possibility of newness, of regeneration, a widening of our span of pain and joy. A human fact, completing and most closely linked with those other human facts, the vocation to service, to beauty, to truth. A fact, then, which must control our view of personal self-discipline, of education, and of social effort: since it refers to the abiding Reality which alone gives all these their meaning and worth, and which man, consciously or unconsciously, must pursue.

And last, if we ask as a summing up of the whole matter: *Why* man is thus to seek the Eternal, through, behind and within the ever-fleeting? The answer is that he cannot, as a matter of fact, help doing it sooner or later: for his heart is never at rest, till it finds itself there. But he often wastes a great deal of time before he realizes this. And perhaps we may find the reason why man—each man—is thus pressed towards some measure of union with Reality, in the fact that his conscious will thus only becomes an agent of the veritable purposes of life: of that Power which, in and through mankind, conserves and slowly presses towards realization the noblest aspirations of each soul. This power and push we may call if we like in the language of realism the tendency of our space-time universe towards deity; or in the language of religion, the working of the Holy Spirit. And since, so far as we know, it is only in man that life becomes self-conscious, and ever more and more self-conscious, with the deepening and widening of his love and his thought; so it is only in man that it can dedicate the will and desire which are life's central qualities to the furtherance of this Divine creative aim.

---

1. "The Mirror of Eternal Salvation," Cap. 7.
2. A good general discussion in Tansley: "The New Psychology and its Relation to Life," Caps. 19, 20.
3. Aug. Conf., Bk. X, Cap. 27.
4. Blake; "Jerusalem."
5. "Social Psychology," Cap. i.
6. "The Interior Castle": Sleuth Habitation, Cap. IV.
7. "The Adornment of the Spiritual Marriage," Bk. II, Cap. 44.
8. Warren: "Buddhism in Translations," p. 28.

PRINCIPAL WORKS USED OR CITED

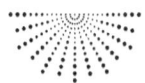

- *S. Alexander*. Space, Time, and Deity. London, 1920.
- *Blessed Angela of Foligno*. Book of Divine Consolations (New Mediæval Library). London, 1908.
- *St. Thomas Aquinas*. Summa Contra Gentiles (Of God and His Creatures), trans. by J. Rickaby, London, 1905.
- *St. Augustine*. Confessions, trans. by Rev. C. Bigg. London, 1898.
- *Venerable Augustine Baker*. Holy Wisdom, or Directions for the Prayer of Contemplation. London, 1908.
- *Charles Baudouin*. Suggestion et Auto-suggestion. Paris, 1920.
- *Harold Begbie*. William Booth, Founder of the Salvation Army. London, 1920.
- *William Blake*. Poetical Works, with Variorum Readings by J. Sampson, Oxford, 1905.
- —Jerusalem, edited by E.R.D. Maclagan and A.E.B. Russell. London, 1904.
- *Jacob Boehme*. The Aurora, trans. by J. Sparrow, London, 1914.
- —Six Theosophic Points, trans. by J.R. Earle, London, 1919.
- —The Way to Christ. London, 1911.
- *St. Bonaventura*. Opera Omnia. Paris, 1864-71.
- *Bernard Bosanquet*. What Religion Is. London, 1920.

- *Dan Cuthbert Butler*. Benedictine Monachism. London, 1919.
- *St. Catherine of Siena*. The Divine Dialogue, trans. by Algar Thorold. London, 1896.
- The Cloud of Unknowing, edited from B.M. Harl, 674, with an Introduction by Evelyn Underhill. London, 1912.
- *G.A. Coe*. A Social Theory of Religious Education. New York, 1920.
- *Benedetto Croce*. Æsthetic, or the Science of Expression, trans. by D. Ainslie. London, 1909.
- —Theory and History of Historiography, trans. by D. Ainslie. London, 1921.
- *Dante Alighieri*. Tutte le Opere. Rived. nel testo da Dr. E. Moore. Oxford, 1894.
- *Abbot Delatte*. The Benedictine Rule. Eng. trans. London, 1921.
- *John Donne*. Sermons: Selected Passages, with an Essay by L. Pearsall Smith. Oxford, 1919.
- *Meister Eckhart*. Schriften und Predigten aus dem Mittelhochsdeutschen. Ubersetzt und herausgegeben von Buttner. Leipzig, 1903.
- *John Everard*. Some Gospel Treasures Opened. London, 1653.
- *George Fox*. Journal, edited from the MSS. by N. Penney. Cambridge, 1911.
- *Elizabeth Fry*. Memoir with Extracts from her Journals and Letters, edited by two of her Daughters, 2nd. ed. London, 1848.
- *Edmund Gardner*. St. Catherine of Siena. London, 1907.
- *Gabriela Cunninghame Graham*. St. Teresa, her Life and Times. London, 1894.
- *Viscount Haldane*. The Reign of Relativity. London, 1921.
- *J.O. Hannay*. The Spirit and Origin of Christian Monasticism. London, 1903.
- *F.H. Hayward*. The Lesson in Appreciation. New York, 1915.
- *F.H. Hayward and A. Freeman*. The Spiritual Foundations of Reconstruction. London, 1919.
- *Violet Hodgkin*. A Book of Quarter Saints. London, 1918.
- *Harold Höffding*. The Philosophy of Religion. London, 1906.
- *Edmond Holmes*. What Is and What Might Be. London, 1911.
- —Give me the Young, London, 1921.

- *Baron Fredrick von Hügel.* The Mystical Element of Religion. London, 1908.
- —Eternal Life: A Study of its Implications and Applications. London, 1912.
- —Essays and Addresses on the Philosophy of Religion. London, 1921.
- *Jacopone da Todi.* Le Laude, secondo la stampa fiorentino del 1490. A cura di G. Ferri. Bari, 1915.
- *William James.* The Varieties of Religious Experience. London, 1902.
- *William James.* The Will to Believe and other Essays. London, 1897.
- —Principles of Psychology. London, 1901.
- *St. John of the Cross.* The Ascent of Mount Carmel, trans. by David Lewis. London, 1906.
- —The Dark Night of the Soul, trans. by David Lewis. London, 1908.
- *Sir Henry Jones and J.H. Muirhead.* The Life and Philosophy of Edward Caird. Glasgow, 1921.
- *Rufus Jones.* Studies in Mystical Religion. London, 1909.
- —Spiritual Reformers in the Sixteenth and Seventeenth Centuries. London, 1914.
- *Julian of Norwich.* Revelations of Divine Love, edited by Grace Warrack. London, 1901.
- *C.G. Jung.* The Psychology of the Unconscious. London, 1916.
- *Kabir.* One Hundred Poems, edited by Rabindranath Tagore and Evelyn Underhill. London, 1915.
- *Thomas à Kempis.* The Imitation of Christ: the Earliest English Translation (Everyman's Library). London, n.d.
- *S. Kettlewell.* Thomas à Kempis and the Brothers of the Common Life. London, 1882.
- *William Law.* Liberal and Mystical Writings, edited by W. Scott Palmer. London, 1908.
- *W.P. Livingstone.* Mary Slessor of Calabar. London, 1918.
- Journal Spirituel de Lucie-Christine. Paris, 1912.
- *W. McDougall.* An Introduction to Social Psychology, 9th ed. London, 1915.
- —The Group Mind. Cambridge, 1920.

- *W.M. McGovern*. An Introduction to Mahāyāna Buddhism. London, 1921.
- *Mechthild of Magdeburg*. Das Fliessende Licht der Gottheit. Regensburg, 1869.
- *Reynold Nicholson*. Selected Poems from the Divāni, Shamsi Tabriz. Cambridge, 1898.
- —Studies in Islamic Mysticism. Cambridge, 1921.
- *J.H. Overton*. John Wesley. London, 1891.
- *William Penn*. No Cross, No Crown. London, 1851.
- *Plotinus*. The Ethical Treatises, trans. from the Greek by Stephen Mackenna. London, 1917.
- *Plotinus*. The Physical and Psychical Treatises, trans. from the Greek by Stephen Mackenna. London, 1921.
- *J.B. Pratt*. The Religious Consciousness; a Psychological Study. New York, 1921.
- *Richard of St. Victor.* Opera Omnia. Migne, Pat Lat., t. 196.
- *W.H.R. Rivers*. Instinct and the Unconscious, Cambridge, 1920.
- *Richard Rolle of Hampole*. The Fire of Love and Mending of Life, Englished by R. Misyn (E.E.T.S. 106).London, 1896.
- *Bertrand Russell*. The Analysis of Mind, London, 1921.
- *John Ruysbroeck*. The Adornment of the Spiritual Marriage, the Book of Truth, and the Sparkling Stone, trans. from the Flemish by C.A. Wynschenk Dom. London, 1916.
- —The Book of the XII Béguines, trans. by John Francis. London, 1913.
- *R. Semon*. Die Mneme, 2nd ed. Leipzig, 1908.
- *Herbert Spencer*. Education: Intellectual, Moral, and Physical London, 1861.
- *B.H. Streeter and A.J. Appasamy*. The Sadhu: a Study in Mysticism and Practical Religion. London, 1921.
- *B.H. Streeter*. (edited by). The Spirit: God and His Relation to Man. London, 1919.
- *Blessed Henry Suso*. Life, by-Himself, trans. by T.F. Knox. London, 1913.
- *Devendranath Tagore.* Autobiography, trans. by S. Tagore and I. Devi, London, 1914.
- *A.G. Tansley*. The New Psychology and its Relation to Life London, 1920.

- *St. Teresa*. The Life of St. Teresa written by Herself, trans. by D, Lewis. London, 1904.
- —The Interior Castle, trans. by the Benedictines of Stanbrook, 2nd ed. London, 1912.
- —The Way of Perfection, ed. by E.R. Waller. London, 1902.
- Theologia Germanica, ed. by Susanna Winkworth, 4th ed. London, 1907.
- *Soeur Thérèse de l'Enfant-Jésus:* Histoire d'une Ame. Paris, 1911.
- *Francis Thompson.* St. Ignatius Loyola. London, 1909.
- *W.F. Trotter.* Instincts of the Herd in Peace and War, 3rd ed. London, 1917.
- *Miguel da Unamuno.* The Tragic Sense of Life in Men and in Peoples, Eng. trans. London, 1921.
- *Evelyn Underhill.* Jacopone da Todi, Poet and Mystic. London, 1919.
- *C.B. Upton.* The Bases of Religious Belief. London, 1894.
- *J. Varendonck.* The Psychology of Day-Dreams. London, 1921.
- *H.C. Warren.* Buddhism in Translations. Cambridge, Mass., 1900.
- *John Wesley.* Journal, from original MSS. Standard edition, vols 1-8. London, 1909-16.

ALSO BY EVELYN UNDERHILL

ISBN PAPER: 9782357284678 HARDCOVER: 9782357284678
E-BOOK: 9782357284562

ISBN PAPER: 978-2357285231   HARDCOVER: 9782357285231
E-BOOK: 9782357284579

ISBN PAPER: 9782357285835   HARDCOVER: 9782357285842
E-BOOK: 9782357285859

ISBN PAPER: 9782357286993   HARDCOVER: 9782357287006
E-BOOK: 9782357287013

Copyright © 2021 by Alicia Editions
Credits: Canva
All rights reserved.
No part of this book may be reproduced in any form or by any electronic or mechanical means, including information storage and retrieval systems, without written permission from the author, except for the use of brief quotations in a book review.